LIVING
BREATHING
SPIRIT

Tony & Ann Turner

To our Dearest friends Gloria
and Terry, we look forward
to your next visit.
Gods blessings always be
yours
        Loads and loads of love
Big Hugs ×xx   Ann, Tony

Con-Psy Publications

First Edition

© Tony & Ann Turner

2009

Published by
CON-PSY PUBLICATIONS
P.O. BOX 14,
GREENFORD,
MIDDLESEX, UB6 OUR

ISBN 978 1898680 48 2

Printed in Great Britain

CONTENTS

Dedication

We dedicate this book to all our spirit loved ones, family and friends, and especially you Mum; there are no words to express our feelings We love you so much.

Acknowledgements

Firstly we give thanks to all spirit people, for their guidance and inspirational thoughts.

We would like to take this opportunity to thank the many friends and acquaintances who have freely given their time and patience, with love and harmony for without them this book would never have seen the light of day.

The following:
Chang Spiritual Guide
My brother Jim
Karen and Marcia daughters
Corrina granddaughter
Charlie our best friend
Shozo Japan
Sandy and family, Australia
Brenda from London
Karen from Ashford
Thelma from Cornwall
Evie from Middlesex
Sandie from Kent
Patsy, Paul and all family, Kent
Harry, Australia
Alison and Simon, Kent
Fred from Kent
Robert from Kent
Josie and family from London
Joan from Crawley
And all our animals

CHAPTER I

Ann born

To friends wishing you well and happy reading

'On March the 31st 1943, right in the middle of the second World War, Veronica Ann was born, that's me five pound three ounces of mothers pride (makes me sound like a loaf of bread) not so sure about that! The bombs were dropping outside but no-one could hear them above my vocal chords if anything I always had a good set of lungs. The staff at Park Royal Hospital London just smiled and comforted my mum.

First Spiritual experience

I can not say I remember my first encounter with human life but I do remember my first encounter with spirit life. I was about two and a half years old at the time, and had woken from my sleep, and what a fright I got, also my mum as you can just imagine, with my screaming.

It had been a hectic day, getting up to all sorts, and keeping my mum on her toes as usual. That night I awoke to see a very bright glowing white light at the foot of the bed. I slept with mum in those days as Dad was away in the Royal Air Force. He was six foot tall, a handsome Irish man who looked like a gentle giant to me.

We lived in a very old terraced house in Willesden NW10.Our house had been converted into two flats, and upstairs lived a lady by the name of Mrs Good. We had the ground floor flat which consisted of three rooms, also a kitchen, scullery and a toilet out the back with lots of creepy crawlies. Another lady by the name of Mrs Marshall had one of our three rooms, and I remember her well. She was always telling us kids off in the street, and we used to call her an old witch, little did I know then but that name among others would be with me throughout my whole life, and still is.

Saw my sister Eileen

Getting back to that night, the glow I saw seemed to fill up the whole room, from wall to wall, everywhere was bathed in the brightest white light my first thought was that mum had lit the candle, but looking over I could see she was fast asleep, besides the light was to bright to come from a candle. Suddenly there was this little girl, sitting at the bottom of the bed, her whole being was radiating, I was fully awake then, I can not remember much more about that night except my mum cuddling, and kissing away my cries and fears until I went back to sleep. In the future years mum told me that the little girl was my sister Eileen who had died of meningitis of the spine when she was three years of age or there abouts, and that now she was in heaven. I was just a tiny baby in arms when my brother Jim, and sister Eileen were evacuated to families up north, and so at my young age I was not really aware of having a brother or sister.

Anne at age 4 years

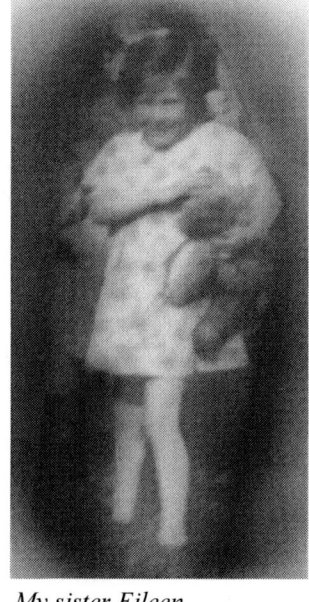

My sister Eileen

My lovely Mum

My brave mum

My mum must have been very sad during those terrible war years as I imagine was the whole of the UK, to have two of her children living so far away from home but her motherly love never waned despite the miles, and such a long time apart. If anything, circumstances increased her yearning, and so she would visit them at every possible opportunity, somehow scrapping together the train fare and tolerating the lengthy and hazardous wartime journey.

During the air raids mum used to put me under the kitchen table with her when the bombs were dropping, sometimes she used to take me to the air-raid shelter at the bottom of our garden. The same shelter was also the source of many childhood memories when I was older, friends and I would play in it and wear the gas masks in there, they were made of black rubber with a glass nose and eye piece, we had a cellar where the coal was kept and that's were mum stored the gas masks on hooks, long after the war had finished. Returning to that little girl on my bed, after seeing her that first time she would always come back when I was alone and playing with my dolls, and we would talk and play for hours. Although mum had told me Eileen was my sister I did not of course understand that she was in heaven and indeed where was heaven? As it was always put, sometimes I used to cry for Eileen to be with me, and when she did come and play I never wanted her to go away again but she always seemed to go. It was not until I was much older that I understood why.

Growing up with the companionship of my sister and playing and talking to her was natural, my friends in the street did not seem to quite understand. I mentioned earlier about Mrs Marshall and one of the names we called her, well quite frankly, names such as witchy and nutcase and many others they also called me, but I was never really bothered. In fact I thought my friends were odd because they did not have a sister who visited from the spirit world who was their friend and could share lots of fun and laughter, they were odd not me, my mum understood the both of us. She was always telling me never to be afraid of spirit people, saying "they will never hurt you it's only the human race on earth that hurts you" and so life went on. I have often had cause to remember her words of wisdom and advice over the years. Thinking about my dear sister Eileen, I sometimes wonder what life would have been like for me had she not quietly slipped into the spirit realms. Writing about having my sister with me for all these years now, may perhaps sound odd, I feel that more guidance, love and strength has been gained from her than possibly would have been if, she had not gone into the spirit realms and I feel we are closer, almost like a second skin, after all she may have married and we could have drifted apart and even lost touch as so often happens, I feel the same about all spirit family and friends. I can not imagine them never being with me and consider myself very privileged indeed, and add here thankful to God for allowing one of his children, my sister to be beside me since that very young age of two and half.

You may wonder how I can be so sure about the age, well the war ended in 1945 or there about and my dad came home from the R.A.F and Jim came back to London from the north of the country, we were one big happy family again no more hiding under the kitchen table or running out to the air-raid shelter for mum, and I.

Looking back to our terraced house in Willesden where we lived for many years many, many happy years with lots of very fond memories that are still with me, even though it was bread and dripping for tea most days, by the way I still indulge now and again especially when roasting a nice lamb joint. Mum always asked Jim and I every day "did you eat all your school dinner?" yes! Yugs! a little white lie never hurt anyone, school dinners were really horrible with those lumpy mashed potatoes, and custard so thick you couldn't even push through to find what was likely to be lurking underneath; truthfully I ran all the way home from school just to have my bread and dripping. Yummy! Yummy!

We didn't live very far from our local school although it seemed then that our street was very long, however a few years ago whilst visiting my Mum we took a detour and drove right past our old house and do you know the road didn't seem half as long, all those lovely happy, and yes sad memories came flooding back, quite overwhelming, you would think I would want to put my young life behind me, but not me, you see those young years were the beginning of a very happy life and spiritual pathway, never ending, always going forward and onto greater things and so many happy hours spent meeting with and talking to spirit friends how humble I feel to know them all. No matter what has ever happened, and there have been times when I wondered how I could possibly carry on they have always inspired and helped with little loving, inspirational thoughts.

Here I am now truly going into older age, quite unbelievable the life so far, sitting writing these words. Tony my husband is reading the newspaper, Max our Doberman dog asleep on his chair, Tabs, Sunny, and Ayesha they are our family of cats asleep on the radiator all of us in our snug little terraced house in Kent, yes our house very much like my parents home where I lived as a young girl in London, why even my brother Jim made comment on the similarities when visiting.

Mind you, we don't have an old tin bath like we did back then, I remember those bath nights so well, or should I say scrubbing nights. Mum just loved to get the old tin bath out and fill it up from our blue boiler, even that boiler brings back memories.

Jim and I always seemed to go looking for dirt on bath nights; we used to come home black, like a couple of chimney sweeps.

Do you know that when the roads were first tarmacked we were told that tar was good for you, so all us kids in the street, and I mean all used to chew it as if it were chewing gum! So even our teeth were black, no wonder Mum couldn't wait to get us in the bath, and no wonder our teeth started to fall out, what kind of old wives tale was that? No wonder my generation all seem to have false nashers.

It was set down on the scullery floor, and then came out the funny smelling green carbolic soap, what a smell that was like poo, yugs, and we didn't have nice soft sponges either, it was a hard scrubbing brush! our skin must have been sore for the rest of the week, I could see my sister Eileen laughing so much on those bath nights, but I could never get angry with her because if I did she wasn't there. Talking about my sister she certainly had the best of both worlds don't you think? But there again so did I.

Jim didn't really take a lot of notice of my ramblings he thought I was just talking to fresh air so to speak, but there we were in the tin bath together, sitting face to face and splashing water all over the floor, until Mum came in and gave us a clout!

Fortunately Mum always seemed to understand spirit people visits; she was really the only person I could talk to in depth during my early years, as it wasn't until I grew up that I realized that there were others like myself with whom many hours would be spent exchanging spiritual experiences.

My Dad was also very understanding, it pleased me so much when they both sat and listened eagerly to my ramblings about spirit people, did I give them an earache.

In those days many people didn't know what it was like to have a telephone and we were no exception communication was mostly by post, or telegram for urgent messages.

My sister was living up north where she had been evacuated to. One night she was suddenly taken ill and she passed the next morning most unexpectedly.

Although our good friend Dr Pollard allowed us to use his telephone and receive the occasional message, it was the police that came to the door to inform Mum of Eileen's passing. It goes without saying that Mum was truly and totally devastated can you imagine the shock? She must have cried and cried untill there were no more tears left. Of course there would have been a brave face to show the world, and yet deep down where the innermost feeling dwell was a silent numbness which the loss of a loved one brings especially ones own little child, also the deep hurt of not being with her to cuddle and hold her close whispering loving words of comfort to her when she suddenly became ill.

Life must have been certainly unbearable; to make matters worse Dad who was needed most in her life at that time of deep mourning was away in the RAF, suffering alone his grief and such turmoil.

My Dad – front row, first left

With Jim still up north and me a tiny baby in arms, who could she turn to?

You may even wonder why Mum and I were not evacuated? The reason she gave was that all the other neighbours and friends in the street, as well as herself wanted to stay together and help each other through the dreadful war, besides all the mothers with young babies were just not evacuated so they stayed at home together it was this friendship and bonding which helped Mum during that dark, dark period in her life

Little did she know then but her strength and courage would again be needed and drawn upon, for within three years our happy family would be shattered and broken once again only my Mums great strength could and did hold the family together as only she could.

Eventually my Dad and Jim came home, the war was finally over and there was peace again! so there we were Mum, Dad, Jim and I one big happy family safe sound and well, or at least that's what we thought! They were the happiest days of my young life.

Mum, far left, Jim and me and all the kids in the street

Dad never abandoned us

When Dad came home from the war all was well for a short while. I remember him so vividly, and have such happy memories of the short time we all had together, simple yet happy memories such as the times he would lift me up to blow out our gas lanterns which were situated high up on our walls.

Sundays were always a very special time for Jim and I, Dad used to take us to the local pub with him, he wasn't a heavy drinker but always enjoyed his pint of Guinness on a Sunday, while Mum was at home getting the dinner ready, we used to sit outside the pub eating our crisps and Dad would let Jim and I have a sip of his Guinness, we never told Mum our little secret. He!He! It was so nice just sitting there, we felt so happy sharing that little hour together, with the warm sun shining down on us as we ate our crisps and drank our lemonade, that was our Sunday we loved Sundays as I am sure Mum did also giving her a bit of peace and quiet with both Jim and I from under feet.

Dad had a very bad cough from which he had been suffering on and off ever since he came home from the R.A.F. I was nearly five at the time and remember well, he stayed in bed quite a lot he could be heard coughing and coughing all over the house it made me so, so sad and miserable to hear him suffering,   *

He slept in the box room, and I used to sit by the bed for what seemed like hours at a time, thinking back now it probably was not so long, as his frailness did not permit long visits. I remember sitting there holding his hand and telling him little stories eventually Dr Pollards visits to him became more, and more regular as the days and weeks went by. You may recall Mrs Marshall who was mentioned earlier she still lived in her room in our house, and seemed to be even more wicked then any old witch ever born every day unless it was very bad weather she would sit outside on the wall at the front of the house always leaving the door wide open oblivious to my Dads serious illness the condition of T.B., letting all the cold wind into the house, remember we did not have central heating I felt in my childlike mind that she was deliberately making my Dad cough making him ill, and I would tell her in no uncertain terms that she was a wicked, wicked lady.

Our next door neighbours Harry and Edie Voice were always popping in to sit with Dad whom eventually became bedridden.

But when sitting with him he always found time and energy to speak loving fatherly words to me and giving me big hugs and cuddles

That horrible, horrible day came a little later when an ambulance arrived to take Dad to the hospital he insisted on walking rather than being carried on a stretcher I walked beside him clutching his hand as we neared the ambulance he turned to my Mum asking her to give Harry Voice the ten bob that he owed him, Harry and Edie were standing on their front doorstep, Dad always borrowed ten bob from Harry and always paid him back on pay day, even in his desperately ill state he didn't forget to pay back what he owed, or was it a knowing that he was about to embark on that little small journey to life everlasting?

He then got into the ambulance, mum there beside him waving goodbye to us all. Jim and I went back into the house to be looked after by Mrs Good the lady who lived upstairs, that was the last time that I saw my Dad alive in the physical sense.

Dad passed into the spirit life a couple of days after the ambulance took him away, I was five years old at the time.

Whilst sitting with him, he always promised he would never leave us, never, and he would always look after us.

As young as I was I knew through my sensitivities that his time was nearing and that he was very soon going to join Eileen in heaven, but I wanted him to stay with us like before. But it was not to be.

Even though Eileen visited often, nothing and nobody could ease that dreadful pain that Mum, Jim, and I were suffering our world had fallen apart, really all I wanted was to be in heaven with my Dad..

There did come that time when we were all together again, but that comes a little later, with a difference.

I was a big girl now and about to start school. The gnawing grief and sharp pain of my Dad's passing then began to ease just a little. Life somehow went on as it does. We all adjusted to our loss and in time developed a routine, after a while Mum, Jim, and I were quite happy.

Mum used to take Jim and I around to see our Aunty Emmy quite regularly and I feel we always visited her on a Saturday. we liked going to see her as she was a nice lady, and always had a big bowl of fruit and sweets we used to sit very quite for what seemed like hours a very difficult thing for two youngsters to do until she asked us if we wanted any goodies YUMMY, yummy.

Aunty Emmy, and Uncle Gilbert lived over the doctors surgery one and the same that had attended to Dad they were Dr Pollards caretakers, he played a large part in our life's he was like a kindly Uncle to us.

On the way home from Aunty Emmy's and just before we went indoors, Mum would point to the sky and say" don't forget to say goodnight to your Dad up there in heaven" I used to call out "goodnight Dad goodnight" I expect the neighbours thought that we were quite barmy, what do you think?

Earlier I told you how Dad said he would never leave us, true to his word and promise one night after Mum had put me to bed, here should be added I often used to wake up to hear Mum as we slept together, speaking to herself and looking towards the big mirror that hung over the fireplace, I felt a little afraid to ask her who she was talking to, as the shock of loosing her young child and husband could be making her do strange things. However curiosity got the better of me, and I nervously asked her "who are you talking to Mum" she simply answered "Your Dad" and that if I were to look at the mirror I would also see him! I did look, and there he was! Mind you just his head and shoulders he didn't talk to me though, only to Mum but it was so lovely to see him again looking so well and not coughing, I knew then that he would keep his promise, I just knew it.

The night it happened, Mum had tucked me up snug and kissed me goodnight, after saying my prayers off I went to blissful sleep no different to any other night. Maybe I had been asleep a few hours I can not say when suddenly I was awoken by a bright light just the same as before, a very bright illuminating white light which lit up the whole room and there he was my Dad a radiant soul, by the side of the bed, standing there right there beside me, it was really him, unbelievable you may think and then he was gone the room looked darker then ever, my sobbing could be heard down the street such tears of happiness, then there was Mum cuddling me back to sleep.

Being only five and a half years of age at the time, you see it did not really take him long to show himself as he had promised.

As the years went by attending many Spiritualist churches etc and sitting for development for physical phenomena of mediumship with a far greater understanding of the knowledge of spirit life, realisation dawned that natural child mediums are born and no I certainly was not a oddball after all.

Whiskers my cat
I liked going to school and being with all my friends but found some subjects a bit boring zzzzzzzzzzz consequently I was a little inattentive, causing my teachers to think me not very bright when it came to some areas of learning. However I made up for it on some subjects which appealed to me, I am sure you can guess what they were. Friends and I were allowed to play in the street after we had eaten our tea. In the late forties there were very few cars about and so there was little danger from them if we occasionally ventured into the road, we used to get up to all sorts of children's games such as knock down ginger, knocking on peoples doors and running away, two balls, which meant juggling them against the wall, and skipping and doing acrobatics.

Me with Whiskers   *and with Blobs*

16

Animals have always played a big part of our family unit and sharing our lives. Childhood was made all the more happy and memorable because of our furry friends they always showered upon us such abundance of love and devotion, of course we loved them dearly in return we always had such fun and would happily while away many happy hours together.

At the weekend I went to the local shops with Mum and used to take my pram, not with dolls in it though but with my cat, whiskers was her name she was a tabby cat just like a little tiger Grrrrr I would dress her in all my dolls clothes, and she never made a fuss, she didn't seem to mind at all she was very, very gentle in fact she really did seem to enjoy it!

When Mum stopped for a chat in the street as often as not to have a little gasbag the person to whom she was talking would ask me how's the baby? looking into the pram, or say what a lovely baby you have, can you imagine their surprise when they saw Whiskers! My cuddly little cat dressed up in dolls clothes she certainly enjoyed all the attention, purrr, lying there all day, (no I did not put nappies on her) even when we went into the shops on the high street, unbelievable! thinking back to those times.

Being a girly cat, she often had kittens (Trollop, always out on the prowl) Mum would let me stay up and watch as Whiskers meow, meow, brought more tiny fluffy handfuls of love into the world she always seemed to choose the night time to give birth and sometimes I would help her if she was having difficulties giving birth, in fact looking back it was probably why Mum liked having me there and perhaps it was then that I first began to use my natural healing abilities, which we all have as natures way, to help soothe and comfort her. We had her from when she was six weeks old and I can never remember not having her, she lived to the grand old age of seventeen.

She had many kittens, once I overheard Mum talking to a neighbour saying that when the kids were in bed she would put the kittens in a bucket of water, and then take Whiskers to the vets and have her spayed, because no sooner had Mum found homes for the latest kittens then whiskers would have some more, I believe everyone in our street, and probably neighbouring streets must have had one of her kittens, and what I am about to write may shock you, there have been lots and lots of prayers to God asking for forgiveness.

One day Mum was outside the front talking to Edie, I filled up a bucket with water, then taking hold of the smallest kitten, a tiny little thing whose eyes were just starting to open; I put it in the bucket of water all the time thinking what a good and clever girl I was being for my Mum.

By this time the kitten lay motionless in the water, what had I done? Feeling absolutely terrible my thoughts all over the place, taking the poor little kitten out of the bucket, grabbing a towel and wrapping the poor little mite, gently cuddling and kissing and rubbing it dry, at the same time praying please please breath with tears running down my face, doing everything I could think of, then came what looked like a little spark of life, a twitch, and movement, sitting there on the scullery floor feeling its breathing oozing life back into its tiny little body words can not express the sorrow and remorse I felt.

All this time Mum was still out the front talking, I did not tell her until many years later about that terrible day, and have never told anyone else since, but now it is in writing you can imagine how I felt. The memory of that day I have carried with me always

The kitten was given a loving, caring home by my Aunty Muriel, he lived until he was twenty five years old a remarkable age for a cat I think the Guinness book of records would agree.

Mum did eventually have Whiskers spayed where upon she lived a long and healthy life.

Those times with Whiskers and her kittens shall always be remembered, for I have always had many cats throughout my life and have always looked upon them as my "babies" and family members, I have always been fond of not only cats but all animals, including those belonging to other people, and I would especially jump at every opportunity to visit friends and family that kept pets, no matter what they were.

Josie, Grans parrot

It's worth a mention here about Josie, one of my child-hood friends that I grew up with she lived across the road, often I would pop over to see her family and her Gran, and in particular her parrot, it was a right natter-box it used to say "Cor blimmey mate" and "hello cocker" and "I love you" etc, I can't recall his name but did enjoy our little chats.

Age eventually catches up, as it did for the natter-box parrot and it simply passed to the spirit life, all us kids in the street loved that parrot and although none of us understood, there he was still on his perch in his cage.

Perhaps you have guessed it? Yes, she had, had him stuffed and mounted. You can just imagine all the love that she felt for her little birdie.

Some years later Josie's Gran also passed, I wondered if she would visit from the spirit life, in fact she did, awhile later I had an astral dream in which Josie's Gran gave proof of after life showing herself with her parrot perched on her shoulder.

I never did tell Josie, for I didn't think then that she would understand, however in the passing years and with many of her loved ones passing to the spirit life, and herself attending many Spiritualist churches, for the ultimate proof of afterlife, she herself has become more aware, I have since discussed with mutual emotion of ones feelings about her Grans visit with her parrot, to say the least this beautiful event gave her much happiness and pleasure and we laughed and laughed with so much joy.

Our neighbour Harry Voice used to fell trees and he some times brought home wild baby rabbits two of which he bought round home for us, we named them Snowy and Blobs they lived out the back by the kitchen door in their little hutch.

In winter time Mum would always bring them indoors into our scullery and guess who had the job of cleaning up their do da's and there were many dropped, but the fun and games we shared with the little rascals that they were, more than made up for their little hic-cups.

At the same time we had Blacky and Tom two of Whiskers kittens, to watch them all playing together was delightful also our grass snake Fred joined in. I cannot remember ever witnessing any squabbles or misbehaving like its dinner time meow. Yummy, our canary Harry would sit on his perch looking on as if to say" tweet tweet let me out to play" so we used to leave his cage door open out he would walk, and he would fly around the ceiling and land on the picture rail that went all the way around the room, it's funny looking back and writing of that time, such memories of loving fun we all had, I can't really say why I have written the last paragraph, are you bored? Yawn, yawn, yawn, perhaps like myself you may have remembered some great fun that you have shared with your pets, how lovely life is.

Mrs Marshall

Whilst I have always had an instant rapport with members of the animal kingdom it hasn't always been so with one or two of the human variety Mrs Marshall was one of them.

When she passed away my Mum had to call in the fumigator because Mrs Marshall wasn't what you would call a clean lady, I had put my very young years behind me, almost forgiven her by now for leaving the doors open and causing the cold drafts when my Dad was so ill. Although it still came into my mind at times, you remember us kids in the street were scared of her when she was alive, looking back now I realise that she was really just a lonely lady, who was getting older, with bad health conditions of her physical body to suffer as we all do in our older age very sad.

Mum used to look in on her every day, as did her gentleman friend by the name of Mr Warren, he was very nice and we kids liked him as he seemed very different to her, still we are all made differently as I discovered many years later, and how different, what a boring life it would be if we weren't.

After Mrs Marshall had passed away, we then had an extra room, yippee! Mum had Mrs Marshall's old room, Jim had the box room and I was in the front room on a put-you-up bed it was pure bliss it felt like heaven, my own room. Even if it was our front room during the day, it was still mine at night, yes.

Things began to change, Eileen didn't visit so often, and Dad only showed himself in the mirror over the fireplace when I thought of him although he was not the only spirit person seen in the mirror and elsewhere.

I could never sleep with a mirror opposite the bed, as I discovered spirit people would keep me awake showing themselves to me naughty, naughty even now I will not sleep with a mirror opposite the bed.

Spirit people often woke me from my sleep, one occasion happened when I was fast asleep in my bed, it was the early hours of the morning and almost daybreak when I became aware of this spirit person walking up to my bed, and guess who? It turned out to be Mrs Marshall it really was her. She looked a little younger but there was no mistake it was her, I reached over and pulled back the curtain in the dawn of that day to make sure that I wasn't just imagining her and needed proof to the contrary, but there was no doubt. Although there was no bright light around her, no glow, I wasn't afraid, just a little apprehensive.

She walked right up to me and uttered only one word "sorry" now as then I have always slept with the bedroom door shut, after speaking she turned around and walked out of the doorway, not through the door, she actually left the door ajar, it is very hard for me to explain what was felt although sadness and regret come to mind, could I have tried harder to understand her more? It seemed to me that it wasn't until Mrs Marshall had passed that she realised what a life she had led, and for her to come through like that, with no bright light only dull like a dark mist, I knew that God had forgiven her, and of course so have I, having prayed for her to go to the light many, many times since.

At eight o'clock that morning when Mum woke me up for school, for confirmation, I asked her if my door was open, she said that it was, when she came to wake me. I always close my bedroom door as I have already said, to me it confirmed it wasn't a dream. I then told my Mum all about my visit from Mrs Marshall, you know I never knew her first name, all adults were called by their surnames back then, she only visited me that one time, and has never shown herself since, to know her life has gone on gives me much happiness, I do think of her now and again and maybe one day she will visit me again maybe, she will show herself in a blaze of bright, glowing light.

Gran, as I called her
Another spirit person I saw was my "Gran" but under totally different circumstances.

You know I used to take Whiskers in my pram when going out to the shops with Mum, this particular morning as we were returning home after our shopping trip.

We found Aunt Doll on her doorstep in a proper state; she wasn't really my aunt but a second cousin who was a lot older then me. Her mum who I used to call Gran had been very poorly, and as I have just said Aunt Doll was in a right state when my Mum asked her whatever was the matter? She was told that Gran "had gone" I knew what that meant, even though I was only seven or eight years of age at the time.

Aunt Doll took us to Grans bedroom where Mum told me to sit quietly on the chair in the corner, for me not to fidget was hard, I did though without making to much fuss. My Mum never gave my presence a second thought because she knew I would not be afraid, and that I understood about passing far more then most grown-ups. So there I sat so quietly you wouldn't have known I was there.

My Mum asked Aunt Doll to bring clean towels and a bowl of water, and some clean sheets; she then placed two pennies over Grans eyes and laid her out.

As I watched Mum and Aunt Doll prepare Gran for the spirit world I became aware of a mist above the bed and then actually saw Gran leaving her old and feeble body, rising up into the mist, thinking at last she had became free of her pains and earthly burdens, having suffered them for some time (months).

There was such a lot of serenity on her face as she rose higher and higher and then sort of dissolved into the mist which then disappeared completely.

Passings are of course times of great sadness and much grief and this was no exception for me, although very sad there was also a sense of elation when seeing Gran actually leaving her physical body. I seemed to know that she was now very happy and going to a place which was full of joy, happiness, and peace, I just knew all this and so I felt happy also.

Dr Pollard arrived, and Gran was later laid out to rest in the front room. Her physical body looked so nice and beautiful, just as she looked when alive and in good health.

As we left Grans we found that Whiskers was still in my pram all curled up and fast asleep, why. She hadn't moved an inch.

CHAPTER 2

My brother Jim and his friends
I have always been very close to my brother. Poor Jim he had to suffer me when I was a little girl.

I phoned him just the other day and we spoke of and remembered much about our childhood days and you know the one thing that still stays with us so strongly in our memory as if it was yesterday is that he used to have me tagging along while Mum was out at work.

There I was his little sister, out with him and his mates; moan, moan, and who could blame him. He would have to take me to the pictures, out to the park, and for bike rides etc.

Thinking about that now makes me feel very sad for him, although we really did enjoy each others company, we were and still are very close, but it is funny the thoughts we all harbour and bring to light after many years.

What with Eileen and Dad passed on, and Mum out working to earn a crust, he must have missed out on most of his childhood having to look after me, his snotty nosed little sister, he being my older brother and Dad all rolled into one. and how very different we are!! we both love each other, and have never pushed our views and opinions, which I feel is very understanding and shows respect for each other's individuality, and most of all free spirit and life, although to my knowledge Jim has never had a spiritual experience in his life

Thinking back to those days, when school had broken up for the holidays always brought much pleasure. Mum was at work, so it meant my big bruv always looked after me, we had endless hours of fun together.

One of our favourite games was when we barricaded the kitchen with chairs, and fired our catapults at each other, guess who always got hurt.

When we used to go to the pictures or flicks as we used to call them, Jim's mate called Michael Brackly sometimes came with us, he was very tall and blonde and I always purposely sat next to him, in my mind I imagined that I loved him, and that one day we would marry and live happy ever after. Of course I was a very young child then who dreamt a lot, but that infatuation was with me until my teens when Michael got married and left the street, and me behind.

Then there was Ba-ba, my friend Josie's brother, his real name was Ian. He was the bully of the street and always beat up us younger ones. One day I was sitting on Josie's doorstep with my friends Margaret and Joan, waiting for Josie to come out and play when Ba-ba appeared eating a really large rosy red apple, and asked me if I wanted a bite, it looked so delicious and inviting I eagerly replied "yes please" but instead of a bite of apple I got a punch on the nose! He not only broke my nose but caused me much pain and suffering for weeks, with constant nose bleeds.

Jim and me

Jim, Jeff and Michael Brackley

Mike, Jim and Michael Brackley

My friends quickly walked me across the road to our house and called my Mum, I don't remember much of what followed except that Mum sent one of my friends with a note to fetch the doctor (Pollard), on arrival he confirmed that my nose was broken and that my blood vessels were ruptured, I had to be kept very still which meant laying in bed with no excitement whatsoever, as you can imagine all of this was very difficult for my Mum as I was such a livewire.

It went on for several weeks with many bleeds before it eventually healed up, my Aunty Kit who was such a jovial soul visited quite often during this time, but when she made me laugh my nose used to bleed so profusely that it was like Niagara Falls, when that happened Mum certainly had her work cut out to stop it. When Jim came home and learned of the incident, he went straight over and sorted out ba-ba which caused much pain to both families, Ba-ba was kept in and his Dad gave him a good hiding, needless to say after that event he was not so much the street bully.

These memories have not been thought about for a very long time, it seems strange thinking about them now and putting them down on paper and perhaps a little unnerving to have such a painful experience recalled, speaking to Josie the other day, we laughed so much recalling that incident.

Aunty Kit and Uncle Tom

My Aunty Kit was married to Uncle Tom, my friends and I used to go to their house in Villiers Road Willesden, some times Uncle Tom used to gave us kids half a crown (12½ pence in new money) not a lot nowadays but then it was a fortune.

Aunty Kit would always have at least three joints of meat to hand, there was always a choice of duck, lamb or beef and she always fed us well, whenever we visited there was lovely cooking smells wafting from her kitchen mmmmmmmmmm. Yummy.

She had a black and white cat called Tiger, he was so big he looked like a Tiger which isn't surprising considering all the joint scraps he used to eat, later in my life he came through from the spirit world to visit me, magic.

Aunty Kit and Uncle Tom lived in my Grandparents house, I never knew my grandparents as they passed on before I was born, my Mum you see was the last of a family of fourteen children, my grandparents have come through from the spirit world many times and so I do know them in a way.

Their house at Willesden was also terraced, and all the furniture was old and dark, Aunty Kit still kept the accordion, piano, double base, gramophone, and a ukulele that once belonged to George Formby she used to play us kids tunes, and we used to have such a great time dancing and singing along, with uncle Tom doing the Irish Jig after a few bevies.

Mum and Aunty Kit

My Aunty Kit

My Grandmother

My Grandfather

I loved that old house, and felt my Grandparents presence on many visits, they often drew close to listen to Aunt Kit playing, in fact "drew close" is not what I meant to say here, for they were there at all times to enjoy the many tunes that she played, of course my friends did not see or feel them as I did, if they did I don't think that they would have visited as often with me, if at all.

It is a very difficult thing to write down, my feelings, looking back to those days, my feelings were of peace knowing my Grandparents were always there, their house was always so warm and loving.

Many years later Aunt Kit and Uncle Tom passed into the spirit world, and although messages were given to me by medium friends, I can not ever remember them coming through to me directly, or showing themselves as most of my family and friends have done.

Of all my Aunties, Aunt Kit was my favourite, and I look more like her then my own mother, and many people used to comment on it, and even now when I look in the mirror I can see Aunt Kit in myself.

As I write these words I come to the realisation that she does show herself, and overshadow me, therefore I thank her for being with me. Its very strange the things we miss in life until putting words down on paper.

Spirit people our neighbours

There was an old Hippodrome in Harlesden where us kids went to play, it had been bombed during the war but a lot of it still stood in all its finery and elegance although it only had half a roof.

There were lots of broken chairs and such like which enabled us to play all kinds of games.

Someone once made a swing from a long thick rope with a big knot on the end and we used to take turns to swing each other, we played in that old building for hours, it was so large we would get lost down the tunnels and corridors, one of our favourite games was to play at being actors and actresses. It was a very hairy scary place, all the kids said that it was haunted and of course it was. When we played hide and seek we saw many spirit people playing with us, and so did some of the other kids which scared the life out of them, I often went there on my own, I loved to roam around that lovely old building, and feel the spirit vibrations.

Looking back to those early days of my childhood, such as the times Mum used to go the pictures with her friend Millie, who we knew for as long as we could remember.

I really liked Millie she was such a happy jolly soul I wonder whats happened to her after all these years? Must remember to ask Mum.

It is such a shame that all contact has been lost considering she played such a big part in our lives, we thought of her as a kindly Aunt.

The nights that Mum went to the pictures are to say the least, and still are very vivid in my mind, as you know Jim used to baby sit, my goodness we did have some fun, as I was often left alone in his care.

Quite often Jim's scout's night would coincide with Mum's and Aunt Millie's well earned couple of hours at the pictures. At times to make matters worse I acted like a spoilt brat saying things such as I'll be alright on my own why don't you go to your scouts meeting obviously bringing the biggest smile to his face but then just as he was getting ready to go out the door I would add, and I will have all your marbles and this weeks coupons or pocket money before you go. (Yes what a little toe-rag I was), much to his disdain he would always hand over, the goodies, and then leg it out the door before I made any more demands.

During my early childhood my sensitivities were less controlled and there were times when I was a little afraid of who might draw close, especially on those scout nights, sitting there counting my marbles all alone my braveness suddenly started to disappear, after all what was the point of material objects when I felt alone and scared stiff,(gulp!)

These times I remember so well, the odd noises, cats wailing out the back in the garden, and walls creak, creak creaking as you know it was a very old house. We did have a nice cosy kitchen, in which stood a big black range, and a nice, very comfortable blue settee, cosy, cosy, cosy.

When Jim left for his scout meetings I would place the two seater settee between the kitchen and scullery door, so I could watch both door handles, scary, were they being turned? Did they just move? I was so scared whilst sitting there my imagination sure played havoc.

Other than my sister and Dad whom I loved very much, and the loving family from that place called heaven, there are others not so nice who often visited from heaven, those spirits were full of mischief and so noisy talk about clank, clank, in the quiet of the night.

In a way my brother was very lucky not seeing or hearing, having no idea at all about the spirit world, don't you think?

When those noises and feelings came about guess what Eileen never seemed to be there to comfort me, it's a wonder that I didn't have a complete breakdown, but I didn't and it made me stronger, to deal with these matters when so very young, and at times completely alone, I feel that I was very brave, don't you?

Mrs Good

She lived upstairs in our house and she was such a nice lady, sometimes I would go up and sit with her. She always gave me a cup of tea and biscuits. Her husband had passed as a very young man, and she often spoke of him. She had a daughter who lived around the comer who didn't visit her very often, in fact not at all. It was so nice to sit and listen to her recount her memories.

When I went off to school in the morning she was always there looking out of her front window waving good bye. On my return there she was waving her welcoming greeting, had she sat there all day? (I think so) she was almost, like a second mum to me.

After she passed the memory of her stayed with me well into my teenage years, I feel it gave her a lot of comfort having a family living in the same house, knowing that she was not alone, she was always very kind although very reclusive and independent. I can not remember her having any visitors apart from my family.

When she became very ill Mum called in Dr Pollard, my thoughts were very mixed in the following weeks, I felt a lot of changes were in store, and yes once again the loss of a dear friend, I was going to miss those cosy chats, cups of tea but especially her warm smile.

Mum used to cook Mrs Good's meals and lay them up on a tray with a rose from our garden which she knew Mrs Good was fond of.

When she became bedridden Mum would help make her comfortable as possible, help to wash, and change the sheets etc.

Mum sent me around to Mrs Good's daughter with a message that her mother was very ill, and still she didn't visit. Sometimes I sat reading her little stories, and it always felt nice and cosy in her company.

My friends often knocked for me to go out and play, they did not understand that I preferred to be with her at those times, my friends used to go off very grumpy with me.

One morning Mum asked me to take Mrs Good breakfast, up to her as I walked up the stairs, and down the long corridor to the landing outside her bedroom all was quiet, too quiet!, I knocked on the door, no answer, I waited, still no answer, listened, then decided to go in.

Truthfully I can state that this was the first time that death of the physical body looked so horrific, she was lying on her back, eyes and mouth wide open as though she had died of shock. Before going downstairs to tell Mum, I said a little prayer, asking GOD to look after Mrs Good in heaven.

For the very last time Mum sent me around to notify Mrs Good's daughter, who then quickly came around to make the arrangements.

Mum took me to the funeral parlour to see Mrs Good laid out; she looked so nice and peaceful then, that I knew that GOD had heard my prayer.

Mrs Good visited many times from the spirit world, for many years we often heard her walking up and down along her hall to the kitchen, and her front room, where she still sat at the window to wave me off to school, and as usual to greet me on my return.

Some may feel when reading this that she was an earth-plane entity, or was this another bout of imagination? All I can say in reply to that, is that she loved her cosy and comfortable home, and us truly, as her very own family and this was her way of looking after us.

Even when Mr and Mrs Swain, who incidentally were Jehovah Witnesses eventually, moved into her flat, we still heard and felt her presence all of the time. When the house was quiet especially when Mr and Mrs Swain (Ann and Bill) were out I heard the floor boards creak, and just knew it was Mrs Good, and felt so safe with her around. This went on until I left home to start on my pathway of married life.

Writing about Mrs Good has brought back more memories of those childhood years, such as the time that Jim and I went out collecting train numbers up at Willesden junction station; this was one of his hobbies. We climbed over the fence next to a bridge onto the grassy embankment, he told me to sit very still, ha!ha! that's a laugh for a start, it was such a steep and dangerous hill.

At this time our Mum was in hospital having an operation to repair a double hernia, and Mrs Good was looking after us, not an easy job

So there we were, me trying my hardest to sit still, and Jim with his binoculars, pen and paper excitedly watching the trains go by and trying to take down their numbers.

Suddenly I found myself rolling down, had I moved? The momentum was taking me faster, and faster down towards the busy railway line, down I tumbled until about halfway down the embankment there was a piece of iron with wire attached to it sticking out. Although yes it did save my life, to which I am very, very grateful, but it went through my left hand between my thumb and forefinger stopping my fall, all the time I was thinking, if the trains don't get me, there's no way I could survive such a steep fall.

At the same time Jim trying to overtake my tumbling and physically stop me as he could see the dangerous descent beneath, when he saw my hand, he pulled it off of the iron bar and wire, blood then shot up into the air like a fountain, quite pretty really, except that it was my blood and not water, it bled that much it covered all our clothes, yuk! Jim was holding my arm straight up trying to stem the flow, it was an impossible task as you can imagine, at the same time carrying me and running like a mad man, well boy! all the way home, I wonder what people that saw us must have thought? I can't recall anyone offering us help, no-one!

We didn't have time to explain what had happened, Mrs Good seeing the seriousness of the situation speedily wrapped a towel around my hand then we were off and running once again to Willesden General Hospital all this time blood was seeping through the towel, amazingly I hadn't bled to death yet! On arrival at the hospital I was taken straight to emergency to see the doctor to have tetanus, and painkilling injections. I can't remember having stitches or the rest of the wire removed, they probably gave me anaesthetic in fact I can't remember the rest of that day. Apparently the doctor said how lucky I was, the outcome could have been far more serious. If you would like to come and see my hand you are most welcome to visit us, I still have the scar.

Even while I am writing this my left hand aches, and I get a numb feeling which as I am left handed causes me problems even today, poor me.

Jim never, ever took me again to collect train numbers, is it any wonder?

Mrs Good who was looking after us, was informed that our Mum was on open order in hospital as she had double pneumonia and pleurisy, and also that at one time her heart had stopped beating; she was in a critical condition Jim and I did not learn of this until much later, poor Mrs Good what must have gone through her mind at that time?

Another memorable incident that comes to mind also features Mrs Good. I arrived home from school one day, and was sent straight to my room without any tea it was very perplexing because she didn't tell me what was going on, it was so unusual, Mrs Good was a very kind and caring lady, later it transpired that the rent man had called, finding the rent card scribbled on she naturally thought that it was my fault, as I was the youngest.

I sat in my room hungry and most angry thinking about it, and the fact that she did not believed me. Later she found the new rent card, and then realized that the one that was scribbled on was in fact an old one, that's when I got a nice treat, goodies! Yummy! I was given my tea with lots of sweets and cuddles as well; it almost seemed worth it, although I wished Mum was home as I missed her so very much.

Spirit were there to comfort and love, lending an ear to listen to my grumbles and mumbles, but no matter what has happened, or what I believe, it would have happened anyway, that's only my opinion life goes on its chosen journey.

Here I would like to mention Mrs Adams who lived across the road, next to the off-licence, she lived in an upstairs room, and like Mrs Good she sat at her window, and waved at all us kids and sometimes threw down sweets, yummy! We would do the odd bit of shopping for her and be rewarded with a couple of pennies.

I feel our generation were more loving, and tolerant towards the elderly understanding their loneliness, unfortunately it is a sad world that we live in today, so lonely and uncaring, has trust been lost? Changes are coming about BIG changes, looking at the world and all the frustration and pain makes me very pleased that I grew up in the early forties, babies aren't babies for long now, and children don't seem to be children for long, hasn't the world changed and the people in it? Where has all the love gone?

Cat Family
Again my cats have just come into my mind, it was my job to feed Whiskers and her two sons, Blacky and Tom and to clear up any accidents they had, and there were quite a few, I can tell you the unconditional love they gave to us all was sometimes better then that received from some human beings. Can you imagine me dressing Whiskers in my dolls clothes; my friends definitely thought I had a couple of screws loose, perhaps I did? So be it if so. Remembering Whiskers now, what a silly dozy cat she was, why she would follow me everywhere and seemed to understand everything said to her, she really did I am sure of it. When I went off to school Mum would have to keep her in, sometimes she would get out, and follow me, my infant school was only down the road and at the times that she did follow me she would sit and wait for me coming out when the bell went, just like a guard dog (cat).

Since her passing we have still shared many good times, she popped along to see us regularly, like all our other furry friends, and to see her, if only for a moment running up the stairs, jumping off the kitchen cupboards, walking out of the wardrobes and playing with our earthly family cats always gives us such pleasure. Now ask yourself, is there a lot of difference between spirit cats and earthly cats? I know without doubt that there is not.

It is overwhelming to know our pets and furry friends do live on in the world of spirit and do share their love for us forever.

Every time we have moved house they have visited, we could feel their presence if not actually seeing them, sometimes a little touch or a fleeting glance, we can always tell when they are around by the reactions of our family cats and the way they play, they seem to enjoy the closeness of there spirit family members, meow.

They often have their moments, especially in the evenings when we are trying to watch a film, DVDs or writing like now, no-one could ever convince me that there is not a spirit animal kingdom the plain facts are that there most certainly is, and all my life I have been given proof in so many different ways, so please my friends, when your pets are about to embark on the journey to the spirit world, and you are sad with grief and pain, remember that the love you share with each other never dies.

I am sure that many of you have had lots of spiritual experiences of not only pets returning, but loved ones as well, perhaps you could phone and let us share together a few! I look forward to hearing from you.

Treasure
Remembering childhood experiences as if they only happened yesterday, such as the particular day when my two friends Josie, Dawn, and I decided to play hookey from school (I played hookey a lot) naughty me! We went to the Welsh Harp in Neasden, a boating lake that was in the shape of a Welsh Harp, there was also a playing field there with swings galore where us kids went to play.

The boats in the lake never came down to the shallow end, and it was only about two foot deep, so we decided to have a paddle, as the day was hot and we needed to cool down, all the times we had visited the Welsh Harp this was our first time for a paddle, so we tucked our dresses into our navy blue knickers, and in we went splashing about feeling the cool water on our legs what great fun, absolutely soaked to the skin!, we had completely forgotten about our clothes, suddenly we noticed something glittering in the water and decided to go further in, getting our clothes even wetter, if that were possible? It was probably an old tin can or something, but that didn't deter us, it started to feel like quicksand, our feet began to sink into the mud but on we went further determined to find the glittering/sparkling object, being a breezeless, and hot sunny day the water was very calm we had no fear of drowning, maybe sinking though! Yuk!

To our amazement the glittering object turned out to be (no not an old tin can) but a coin, it was a half a crown to be exact and we could see many other objects sparkling in the water as the sun caught them, and so we went in even deeper. Great. By this time we were on our hands and knees forgetting everything in our excitement sieving through the mud and weeds as fast as we could, we found many, many more coins all slimy, green and muddy, why you can just imagine what was running through our thoughts, and completely forgetting about the time, we were supposed to be home from school at three thirty. As soon as we had shared out our treasure between us, and what a treasure it was. We ran like the wind home, we ran so fast our lungs were nearly bursting, but being healthy eight or nine years old it wasn't a problem, Mum could see that I had played hookey from school, I think the state of my clothes sort of gave it away. I can't remember what Josie's or Dawns mums said, but my Mum was so relieved that I was home safe (although very muddy and smelly) that she only gave me a small telling off.

After emptying all the treasure into the kitchen sink, (I can still remember the delighted look on Mums face when she saw all the coins) we set about trying to clean them up, how excited we were, and although we couldn't get all the green and corrosion off we did manage to remove enough so that we could see, they were shillings and sixpences, and also they were still legal tender, being a poor family as most were back then this was a bit of a Godsend, Mum was able to go shopping and fill the cupboard up to the brim, and enabling us to have many yummy! treats and goodies for weeks to come, I must phone Mum to see if she can remember that?

Well I did phone Mum, and yes, she certainly did remember, we were on the phone reminiscing for hours, isn't life good?

Could it be that spirit life inspired us kids (well not to play hookey) but to find our wonderful treasure.

The boating lake was cordoned off, I wonder why? Did someone get wind of us kids paddling? And about the coins? Could be some lucky so and so became very rich, what do you think? Just thought maybe Tony and I should break through the fence, and go paddling in the Welsh Harp at Neasden, just to see if we could find any treasure! Those old coins might be quite valuable now, might even see you there some day.

CHAPTER 3

My stepfather (George)

I am sure spirit had a helping hand in bringing my stepfather George into our lives, not once but twice, and both times he played a very different role. At the time I had not long left school, and this particular afternoon I was standing on the step, when a man came out of the house next door. "Hello" he said you must be Eva's daughter? "You won't remember me?" I didn't have time to take a breath, or return his greeting, before he said "when you were a baby in your pram, (ah!) on this very step, I used to put your dummy back in your mouth, it certainly helped all the street get some peace, you did have a set of lungs on you."

His name was George, and I couldn't wait to tell Mum about him when she got home from work, as a cook at the police canteen, you name it! Mum has probably done it! She used to sometimes let me help her in the canteen, I got to know quite a few police officers there, and made many friends at the station.

When Mum came home I told her all about this man George, from next door, he had only moved in a few days before, although he had lived there many years previously "coincidence?" I can't be sure, but it seemed that her face lit up in recognition, and delight, little did I know then, that a year later this stranger would play such a large part in our family life, here and later from the spirit world.

After a few years they got married, and George became my Dad, well stepfather, and best friend, I am sure that my Dad in the spirit life was delighted, for them both.

It had been very hard for Mum, on her own with no husband, and two children to bring up, she would sometimes work day and night to feed and clothe us. I often saw her flop into the chair exhausted. George was there now to look after her, and to make sure she didn't work herself to a standstill!

Poor George, whatever was he letting himself in for, a ready made family, life was a weeny bit hectic for him, (phew) this ready made family certainly gave him a few problems.

But you know, if there is a choice in who you pick as your family I feel we would most definitely been together. I feel this was arranged long before this life.

Stepfather George and Mum at their wedding

Joan Aston and me

Tylney Hall

My Godmother
My teenage years began. I felt these changes, becoming very stubborn, and not learning a thing at my Catholic School despite much urging and patience by the nuns. I was always the one who was called out to stand in full view of the class, for hours on end, or write lines, nobody seemed to understand me, and my so called friends called me names.

They just did not understand my funny odd ways, like "talking to fresh air" they didn't realise I was speaking to my spirit family!

I was so behind with my school work, of course at the time I didn't realise that I was starting adolescence. Leaving my childhood years behind, and growing into adulthood.

There was a house within the school grounds (St Josephs), where a very old lady lived, she kept lots of cats, she lived alone, and may have been the school caretaker?

All the kids called her an old witch (now, where have I heard that before?) I used to knock on her door and ask if I could go into her garden and play with her cats, she had so many, happy, happy me! Thinking back now I can't recall any conversations I had with her, but feel I did tell her about my spirit family, she may of understood. Anyway getting back to what I was writing about, no matter how hard I tried school work just did not interest me at all.

One day I could not answer a question on the catechism, I was called out and in front of the whole class given a good canning, by then it was second nature to me as I was often canned (what a bad attitude I had) Truthfully, I have probably been impossible all my life, but really a nice person, being the first in line to help my friends, lend an ear or be a shoulder to cry on. I used my psychic gifts to help whenever I could and as I grew so did my spirit friends, we were inseparable.

One day Sister Donaghue lost her temper, and gave me the whipping of my life, I ran home in my lunch hour, (naughty me!) I knew that we were not allowed off the school property during break-time, in my haste, forgetting Mum was at work in the police station.

After sitting on the front wall of our house for a while, in order to catch my breath, and wallow in a bit of self pity, for my back and legs felt raw. I set off to my Godmothers house, she lived just around the corner from us, all the time thinking please, please be home, she was! When I showed her my legs and apparently bleeding back she was shocked, and without any ado she took me straight back to school. I was thinking, "Oh no" not back there. I was bound to get another caning for running out of school, but she didn't take me there to stay, she just wanted me close and safe at her side after the horrendous ordeal I had been through, poor, poor me!

With unshakeable determination, she marched straight to her daughter Pat's class, and called her out, we both left school that day never to return!

Mrs Terry (my Godmother) was an Irish lady, and she was fuming, I thought that in her temper she was going to beat up Sister Donaghue the nun who had whipped me, but no she didn't, no-one challenged this stern looking Irish lady when she burst into the class room, the impression that emanated from her, was that no-one was going to harm her daughter or God daughter.

After a while my poor back and legs began to heal, and Mum and Mrs Terry took Pat and I to register at a Protestant school, Pound Lane which was in Willesden, I must say that I did like the school, although I was only there one year I still didn't learn much. Mum was really starting to worry about my prospects. Practically, I was very good at sewing and this was something in my favour, but nought else. I must add here that our other friend Ann Ford also left St Josephs and joined us at Pound Lane school.

I often wondered what became of Sister Donaghue, this day and age there's no way they would have let her teach, or be responsible for children.

Our lives can unexpectedly change direction? Sometimes for the better! And my schooling was just about to take that turn, hmmmmmmm!

Juvenile Court
You will recall earlier in this book reading about the Welsh Harp in Neasden, where Josie, Dawn and I found a lot of coins (treasure) over the coming years we did visit again, no more treasure, one day my friend Val Palmer and I decided to go to the Welsh Harp by bus, this innocent visit was to change my life forever!

On this particular day we had met other friends there, and had a really enjoyable time, when it was time to go home however neither Val or I had our bus fare, perhaps we had lost it when playing on the swings? We noticed a newspaper stall, which had a broken money box on it, so we helped ourselves to sixpence for the bus fare home, naughty girls.

However we didn't get away with it, a man had seen us, collared us kicking and screaming across the road to his newspaper office where he phoned the police. We sat there quiet now, and waited nervously for the police to arrive, when they did they took us away in a black Maria-van.

(No there weren't any handcuffs) I won't tell you the language we used, believe me, you wouldn't want to read it! or hear it! Please remember at this time my life was, and had been changing. I was finding growing up hard

Dad and Eileen didn't visit me so often, can't say I blame them, besides when they were close, they could not change the direction of my life, but only try to help me cope with what happened.

I did feel remorse, and was very upset that I had been neglectful towards those nearest to me; I had let my family down especially my Mum.

When one steps from childhood to womanhood it can be traumatic, and what difficulties one can meet along the way, I had let Mum down, and she had been so loving and understanding, other children were not as naughty as me I am sure. Having Dad to talk to (although in spirit) about this difficult period of my life, must I am sure have helped Mum!

Both Val and I were taken to Juvenile Court, and we each received two years probation, we were also blamed for the other times that the newspaper box was broken into, although it certainly wasn't us! Of course no-one was going to believe us, and my school record, well that wasn't going to impress any one, it was suggested to my Mum that I was sent to boarding school, she agreed that it was probably for the best.

So off I went to boarding school in Hampshire. I must add here that this turned out to be the best years of my school life, the very best! It gave me the strength to cope with life in general and all that it dished out, I thank God for all that I learnt from there.

Although it was only sixpence we took, when writing these words I still feel bad about it, stealing no matter what the reasons is wrong!

Tylney Hall
Thinking back to those years at Tylney Hall, I obviously took some time to settle in. It was a big building which stood in its own grounds, and was surrounded by woods, and the largest, tallest trees, it was very haunting looking, just up my street (lovely) mmmm, more spirit friends, maybe? To greet and talk to, these were the first thoughts that went trough my mind.

Along with others we were driven there in a coach, which was great fun as most of us had never even been in a coach before, we were all given a packed lunch (yummy) goodies! Just like going on holiday.

Feeling miserable, asking myself "why did I take that sixpence?"

Thinking maybe this was meant to be the first of many more bad experiences to come. I certainly hoped not, I didn't realise then but this was the first step of me growing up, but it didn't seem like it then "Why God" we ask when things go wrong in our lives. Chang's (my spiritual guide) answer has always been the same "man causes his own trouble and strife".

Hauntings

I felt so very alone; it didn't help even when my spirit family whispered sweet words to me, I was so sad until I saw Tylney Hall, that lovely old haunting looking building, with its acre's of land to explore, happy thoughts started to emerge!

We were shown to our rooms (dormitories shared by three or four) we unpacked our clothes, and then were told to go to the main hall to meet the head. You know I can't remember his name? Thanks Chang! Mr Kirby was his name, we were lined up and given a talk, lecture more like, there was so many rules and regulations.

Mr Kirby was quite tall and heavily built with a face that looked like a mask smile-less, still we were there to be taught, and in my case to be punished for stealing sixpence and for my cheek, I certainly did have a lot of that and believe me, still have, or so I have been told, nice cheek though.

After that first day the discipline and routine became normal, and although I rebelled and ran away several times I did eventually settle in and make new friends, and Tylney Hall became my new home, yes I did run away, three times in the first six months, the last time sticks in my mind because it was freezing cold and raining, brrrrr!

To be fair though it did have its happy times, especially as it was haunted, yes friends there were many spirit people there, and guess what, other children, and even the teachers, and the house mistress used to see them, feel/sense them so it wasn't that bad after all, and life for me started to take a turn for the better. I learnt more there than at any other school, such as spelling, reading and maths! Although to be truthful maths wasn't one of my best subjects, I loved history, geography, and also sports, and certainly learnt enough to set me on the right pathway in life, I thank my lucky stars for Tylney Hall.

As for the hauntings, or spirit world as we know it, there were tunnels under the school which lead to and from the boys and girls dorms, although of course the entrances were locked, most times anyway the tunnels were long and creepy with lots of cobwebs, yes, to my horror spiders, but that didn't stop us naughty girls, and boys.

When it was very late and our house mistress was fast asleep, and snoring, (we used to listen at her key hole to make sure) we would make an occasional visit to the boy's part of the school to have a meeting, and a crafty fag, puff, puff!

The tunnels were used to store things such as spare bed springs and any other odd bits and pieces. Sometimes the staff when storing stuff forgot to lock the door behind them, hence our little visits, what fun we had thinking our house mistress didn't have a clue, or so we thought? She was so nice and understanding, as though remembering her own childhood or teenage years of course she did know and told me so just before I left there.

Shirley, Lorraine, and Pauline were my dorm friends, we shared everything, those nights we sneaked out we would roll up a blanket, so it looked like we were tucked up fast asleep in our beds, then off we would go down this long flight of stairs to the tunnels, with our little torches.

The first time we saw the couple with their two children, we felt a little apprehensive, apparently they had lived there many years before when it was a country estate (family home) the tunnels used to be their wine storage cellar, can you imagine spirit people indulging in a few glasses of vintage wine? Slurp!

We often saw figures in the halls, corridors and classrooms, and feel Mr and Mrs Kirby saw them too!

After the first few times, we got used to seeing them. In fact thinking back, if the spirit couple didn't appear we would have missed them, yes honestly we would have. Of course it was great fun for me to be able to share my oddities with my friends, and to know that there were others like myself, whom I could share my childhood stories with. Can you imagine how it felt, no longer was I alone I could talk openly and listen to others, spiritual experiences.

The couple were very fond of their home and beautiful gardens, their woods, their orchards apple trees and vegetable gardens.

There was another building on the estate, and I believe that this was used by their staff; mind you it was run-down and becoming a shell of a place, it hadn't been lived in for many years.

We used to love playing in the woods amongst those very old trees, which used to move around in the breeze, and when it rained we would shelter under the long arching branches, the wind going through the trees always seemed to us like whispering voices! It wasn't until many years later that I became aware of the great healing properties, and benefits that can be gained from different trees, just imagine all that healing we must have been receiving although we were unaware of it at the time, all that power they give to us, quite freely it is the most wonderful and exhilarating experience!

Some may find the subject a little difficult to understand, but the countryside hedgerows, wildflowers, grasses and trees are all living things, and vibrant with their own energies radiating through them.

Just consider the mighty oak, every part of this majestic tree is pulsating life giving forces and healing energy, which they are only to willing to impart to us, be at one with nature and graciously except what it has to offer, and you will become more peaceful and also fitter as a result.

It was not just my appreciation of nature that was growing at Tylney Hall but also my psychic abilities, and the realisation that there was a difference between the spiritual, and psychic, we are all born psychic, but not all are born mediums.

Positiveness

Often my friends would have arguments with their boy friends, and as they knew that I was psychic, they would ask "Ann can you do anything to help" or "are we going to get back together?" and then it was usually "will it be today/tomorrow?" I would sometimes be asked "will I get my goody parcel from home as it hasn't come yet?" I always tried to answer as truthfully, and as positively as I was able, because that's the answer folks, always try to be positive, whatever the problem positive thoughts! with truth.

I know that life can sometimes be hard, but believe me positive thoughts do work, although we can't bar cause and effect from our lives, we must remember there is always self responsibility to consider.

It has always been the story of my life to help others, when asked to, obliging no matter what was asked of me, nothing was ever to much, because this is the pathway that I am on with complete enjoyment. "To give is definitely to receive" I learnt that at a very early age, although my life as been long and hard, I really would not change a thing.

Those lovely school years were the best of my life, and thinking back now I wonder if Pauline Lorraine, Shirley, and many others, like myself could be the mediums of today? Surely so! We have probably met on the Spiritualist Church circuits and not even realised it, so if you were at Tylney Hall please, please get in touch, it would be so nice to reminisce those special times with you! ! We could visit Tylney Hall together or even maybe arrange a reunion.

Now this might be a coincidence, the American actor Richard Gere and his great friend the Dali Lama (Tibet) came to England and guess where they stayed? Tylney Hall, which has since my school days, been converted in to an hotel. I wonder if they had a chat with the spirit family that was there, all those years before, by the way we think we still have the newspaper cutting of their stay at Tylney Hall.

You may recall my good friend Josie who I mentioned earlier in this book, well talking to her some years ago on the phone she mentioned that Sara, and Lisa two of her children went with there school,(when they were young), on a camping trip to Tylney Hall, and that while they were there, the word was that the place was haunted, according to the legend they were told a young boy killed himself when it was a school, and that also there was a coachman who roamed the grounds, I wonder if the couple with their two children have been seen? Tony, and I have been talking just recently about booking into the Tylney Hall Hotel for a short stay (well overnight at the prices they charge!) I would love that, all those memories of school days I'm sure would come flooding back, fantastic, obviously giving them a FREE copy of our book!

First employment
After leaving Tylney Hall School I felt quite lost, and missed my friends, and yes! the routine,

It took time to settle, although it was nice to be back home with

Mum, Jim and Whiskas my cat. The years spent at Tylney Hall had certainly changed me, growing up can seem painful at times, I learnt that from my very good friend and teacher "Chang" who said to me "little one, never look back always go forward, life is here and now for you, life is precious, do not waste it".

I was totally unsure of my future at this time, it was obviously necessary to get a job and start earning a living, but I had left school with no qualifications, or skills to speak of. Fortunately I was good at sewing, and that was something at least.

I visited the labour exchange for the first time in my life, quite a grown up daunting experience, help!

They were able to find me a job, my first employment was with Simon & Kentons as a machinist, they were a little firm in Harlesden, the pay was £1, and ten shillings a week, it doesn't seem a lot now, but it wasn't that bad back in the fifties.

After a little while I gradually began to adapt, and feel more comfortable with my life, I was settling down at home, had a job that was enjoyable, and I was getting along nicely with the people I worked with there, especially the spirit lady who seemed to be there all the time, she would be looking over shoulders as if checking our work for mistakes, and laughing when we mistakenly stuck a needle in our fingers (ouch!) which we did often! The saying "it takes many pierced fingers to make a good machinist" is true; we certainly passed that test a few times over.

The spirit lady who was always with us, never revealed her identity to me, she looked about thirty five years of age and was quite elegant looking, I'm not sure if any of the other workers there saw, felt or sensed her, but if they did nobody said so! She was always friendly as she walked around looking at us as we worked, and being able to see her for me was simply magic.

I was happy working there as a machinist, but unfortunately along came the bus strike, and the end of my first real job, the firm closed down as many did at that time

Simon & Kentons used to be situated over a row of buildings, but a big supermarket now stands on the spot. I wonder what happened to the spirit lady? Do you think she might still be there watching over the supermarket staff?

It was about this time that Joan and I decided to go to Moody's Holiday camp.

Moody's Holiday Camp

Joan and I, you will remember she was one of the kids that I grew up with we applied to become seasonal waitresses at a Holiday Camp called Moody's we wrote off and were luckily accepted, we bought material to make skirts, and little tops with, we really were so excited and felt so grown up to be working away from home, and in a Holiday Camp, whoopee! Now don't get bored here, I promise you won't regret reading on. Joan's mother was called Toots, and could she shout, although Joan and I were the best of friends we did sometimes have a scrap, and this was one of those times.

This day I heard Toots at our front door, and as usual, her voice made me quiver, her voice had the same effect on all the kids in the street, I heard my Mum saying to her in a calm voice "kids will be kids, they will be the best of friends again tomorrow" how right she was, but then again she didn't have to replace Joan's torn clothes, I did have a few bruises (ouch!) but they didn't cost money to put right, Mum stopped my pocket money for a week or so, which did help to deter any future tiffs.

To be fair Toots bark was far worse then her bite, she was in fact a very nice lady who I met up with again many years later, whilst on a little visit to see my Mum.

We were shopping in Wembley, and walking along the High Street chatting between ourselves, when we walked past this lady, and her daughter who was pushing a baby in a pram, suddenly this lady grabs my arm and says "You're Ann", well you could have knocked Mum and I sideways, it was Toots and her daughter Jane, Joan's younger sister, imagine that all those years later Toots had recognised my voice! That was when I was at the beginning of writing this book. We had lost contact with Joan and Toots as like ourselves they had also moved. I am sure that spirit engineered this meeting as they knew that I would want to speak to Joan to confirm some of the writings in this book, we made sure that we exchanged phone numbers and addresses.

Getting back to where I was, Joan and I going off to Moody's Holiday Camp, at Hopton on Sea, and feeling very excited as we arrived there. It was only a small camp with about two hundred campers, and only six of us waitresses, lots of hard work ahead, lovely.

We were interviewed, told of our duties, and shown our sleeping quarters, which was in an old Nissen hut-type shelter, which was divided into three bedrooms, with two sharing, unfortunately we only had cold water bimut, as the hot water geyser had broken down! There was also lots of cobwebs, and creepy crawlies (spiders), yugs, my favourite creatures (I don't think!)

We certainly have cause to remember that shelter, as not only was it our home for a time, but Joan and I shared a few spooky happenings there.

Each room had its own little window, although we couldn't see out of it without standing on a chair, the rooms were very sparse, and the walls were made of metal which made them feel extremely cold, brrrr! I really don't remember us having any form of heating; still we were young and healthy, and on this great adventure, with no parental supervision, great, nothing, and nobody could spoil it for us, or so we thought?

We had been working there a week or so, when strange things started to happen, like unseen hands touching us as we entered our bedroom, it felt like walking through invisible cobwebs, it was so cold in there that you would think it was the month of October, not May, we could actually see our breath turn into condensation as we spoke! The other girls there didn't seem to notice any of this; perhaps they did, but were afraid that someone would laugh at them if they said anything, mind you that's the story of my life. Oh yes! the spirit world was most definitely at play, there was plenty of activity, maybe more then one spirit being, we didn't like to feel this cold, it wasn't very comfortable at all.

Apart from that we were having a great time, and enjoying ourselves at the Holiday Camp, little did we know then, our stay was going to be memorable for less then pleasant reasons.

The first time that something happened, was when we had been on our feet twelve long, long hours, and felt very tired indeed, the only thing on our minds was getting to our beds, and sleep! *Zzzzzzzzzzzzzz*! As soon as we returned to our sleeping quarters, it was "goodnight" to the other girls, whose names I can't recall at the moment, but if you are reading this, and were one of the girls that work at Moody's with us, it would be so nice to hear from you.

I don't know how long we had been asleep, but suddenly my eyes were wide open and there walking around our room was a very old lady, she seemed to be searching for someone, it came to me that in her dilemma she hadn't noticed me. My eyes were glued to her, watching her slowly move as she searched, it was as if she knew every dark corner of the room, and her face looked very sad, I got the feeling from her, that she was lost, poor soul!

My thought now was, could it be a camper that had wandered in? No this definitely was a spirit lady, she had passed away and hadn't realised it yet, I asked her who she was looking for? But she didn't answer me, did she even see me I wondered? The light of the moon was shinning through the window, and lit up every detail of her face, and I could even see the colour of her clothes!

Poor Joan

I continued to watch and was quite mesmerised by this sad old lady, when suddenly I nearly jumped out of my skin, I had forgotten my friend Joan, until she shouted (screamed, more like) "Ann, who's that old lady, what does she want?" Or words to that effect! "Put the light on" Joan screeched hysterically. Not much more of that night comes back to my mind, except cuddling each other back to sleep; unfortunately in the panic we didn't see the going of the old lady, I think the screams, probably frightened her, as much as it did me, and she left there sharpish!

The next morning we were up bright and early 6.00am ready for our days work, not that we felt much like it! The other girls didn't mention anything about that night, so we thought it best to keep it to ourselves.

After I explained to Joan that the lady was a spirit person she seemed to be quite calm, mind you we did have a hard day's work ahead of us, so there wasn't really time to think about it!

That evening after work we had another chat about what had happened, poor Joan it brought back all the feelings of fear and who could blame her? That night we decided to sleep together in Joan's bed for security and peace of mind.

That night I will try and write about now

I was once again awoken from a deep sleep, to see the old lady!, this time she didn't look lost and sad, but was staring, and looked evil and very angry the temperature in the room was even colder, if that were at all possible (it's a wonder Mr frostbite didn't step in) a drop in temperature is not unusual when there is spirit activity, but this was extreme! My next recollection is of jumping up on the bed, and trying to escape through the small window momentarily forgetting all about Joan who was beneath my scrambling feet, that idea was soon abandoned, in a flash I was off the bed and heading for the door, my only thought was to get out now. After making it to the door and fumbling in the dark (it seemed like eternity) like a crazy person, I found the handle and was out of that room, I ran out onto the grass verge that the campers used as a play area, yes, running for my life with the old lady at my heels, can you imagine me actually running away from a spirit person? Believe me it was the first time in my short life!

Reality then dawned on me, I came to my senses so to speak I started to realise that I was outside in the open, cold dark night, alone!

Taking a deep breath I decided to go back in, (brave or what?) and I knocked on the other girls doors looking for Joan, because in my panic I thought that she had run out of there before me, however no-one opened their doors which made me wonder if madness was starting to creep in at such a young age!

Still concerned for Joan I returned to our room, my feet were covered in mud, yuk! Cold water wash for me then, before getting back into a nice warm bed, then I heard a whisper, just audible "Ann is that you? Please answer me" I switched on the light, and saw Joan buried deep under the covers, she was shaking quite uncontrollably, it is impossible to express our emotions we felt that night as you can well imagine we were more then terrified. Joan, from the sanctuary of her bedcovers nervously went on to explain that some one had been jumping and stamping on her, (ooops!) and she thought it must be the old lady from the night before, after calming her down, with a feeling of relief we started to laugh hysterically, we almost crack our ribs!

We decided to leave the light on for the rest of the night, what little there was left of it, we couldn't go back to sleep, no way and talked our tongues off until day break, we decided that night to hand our notice in, quit our jobs and leave for home, sweet blissful home!

Joan was in a terrible state over the nights events, and I was very confused having not experienced any thing like this before, although not realising it then, was this simply another pathway for me to experience? Gaining the knowledge of Spirit people, who had perhaps passed, and didn't realise it, or those who had passed in tragic circumstances, with Chang's patience, guidance and teaching I would learn how to help such souls, I do thank God and Chang for allowing me to be used as that channel.

The following years were like being back at school Chang was teaching me so much, well it wasn't quite like school, he was always kind, considerate, and loving, although he definitely did need patience with me I can tell you!

When we were up and dressed we went to see Mrs Moody and explained to her what we both had experienced over the last couple of nights, we probably looked like, and sounded, as if we were having a nervous breakdown.

To our amazement she not only seemed to understand, but also seemed to know about the happenings in the shelter, had she been told about the lady from others that had stayed there before us!

After a long chat she came up with a solution, and asked us if we would stay if other accommodation was found, because she said that she did not want to lose two of her best waitresses. We agreed that we would stay if and only if other accommodation was found for us, but I know we both felt like we should just get the hell out of there!

After packing our bags we met Mrs Moody in the main building, at the reception area, we were so both relieved to be away from that spooky shelter, she took us to the home of one of her friends, who lived within walking distance of the Camp.

The friend of hers turned out to be a elderly gentleman, he was standing on the steps at the front of his bungalow, waiting to greet us and had a big beaming smile on his face, he showed us our room with twin beds in it, and I remember thinking how pretty it was, so different from our room in the shelter, and the other bonus, no creepy crawlies! We then had a nice cup of tea, and were given the rest of the day off so we could unpack and catch up on lost sleep, we were exhausted!

Our host was such a nice man, quite tall and had white hair. When we told him what had happened to us he didn't seem surprised at all, as we thought he would have been. I wonder why not?

He lived on his own after losing his wife some years earlier, and said that us being there, was just what the doctor ordered, as he said we were good company. I don't remember him having any visitors while we were there. He told us to treat the place like our own, it was like home from home to us and we did enjoy the rest of our stay. He always made us feel so welcome. And nothing was too much trouble for him, in fact on our first morning there he offered us grilled eggs on toast, we had cereal from then on.

The other girls were a bit put out that we had been moved, but Mrs Moody asked us not to tell the other girls about the two horrible nights we had, we didn't want to talk, or think about it anyway as far as we were concerned they were best forgotten about

The lesson I took away from that time was to control my emotions, a valuable lesson, to be in control, and not to be controlled!

I feel all matters concerning spirit, help us to live our lives, and know in our development, when to stand back and observe, which is hard sometimes as in this life there is so much pain and suffering. At least we can be thankful that we know life does go on, and there is a world where all our families, loved ones, and animals dwell. They will know when it is time for us to shed this overcoat (physical body) and leave the pain and suffering behind, and join them all they will be waiting, how wonderful.

To those who may read these words share your love with the many people who do not understand life everlasting, share hope, try to help restore that little spark of light that so many lose somewhere throughout their lives.

Regent Palace Hotel

Working at the Regent Palace Hotel in Piccadilly London meant enjoying yet another spirit experience.

What a lovely hotel, so big and grand, I worked there as a trainee silver service waitress, which certainly had its moments. Even our red and grey uniforms were very elegant and a lovely red rose for our hair you know as I write this there is such clarity that it feels like yesterday when this spirit occurrence took place.

This particular morning I was running a little late, and decided to go the quick way, the out of bounds spiral staircase, as you know they wind up, up, and up, on the way up running, puffing short of breath,

Regent Palace Hotel, Piccadilly

to many ciggies! I was desperately willing my aching limbs on, all the time thinking how important it was to be on time, as to be late, meant instant dismissal!

It was an early shift, and travelling to Piccadilly from Willesden meant taking the tube with two changes, also getting up at 5.30am was not one of life's pleasures for me, thinking back now I must have been mad to take a job that was so far away.

Now where was I, oh yes, still running up that spiral staircase, apart from the travelling drawbacks, it was a good job paying £3-10 bob per week plus tips, I felt rich, and also got to wait on some celebrities, what fun that was, their names escape me at the moment, but who knows maybe they recall little old me, the waitress who nearly served tea into their laps, well almost!

Back to my trudge up that staircase each step was getting harder but I pushed on when suddenly I felt a hand on my shoulder, my mind was in a whirl, who was it? What could I do? There was no escape, then came the thought "Ann you've been caught red handed" o'dear I am in big trouble, on turning around quickly, which was quite difficult as you can imagine on spiral stairs my whole body jerked (ouch!) and I felt a pain in my side. Then I saw him, this spirit man who was looking at me all concerned, the pain must have shown on my face, I didn't feel afraid of him at all, a little shocked, but not afraid.

This spirit man on the spiral staircase was at my side, his smile was so warm and comforting, he was positively beaming at me, and never have I forgotten his face and smile, how privileged we are to be helped and guided by those who visit us from the world of spirit. After awhile he suddenly went as quickly as he had appeared, with me still running trying to get to the top and through the kitchen door to the carving room floor, puffing like an old bull, and my heart going twenty to the dozen. You will be pleased to know that I did make it and set about laying up the tables ready for the breakfast rush, with my mind going back to that spirit gentleman, as you can imagine, lovely!

A couple of hours passed, and the pain started to grow worse, it must have been showing on my face as the head waiter enquired about my health, the next thing I can recall was being taken to hospital, and after having an x/ray it was confirmed that I had three fractured ribs ouch! "So much for using the spiral staircase and meeting that spirit man!"

My injury kept me off work for about six weeks, luckily I was on full pay (no tips though) even after I returned to work I was still a bit poorly, and made sure that I never used those out of bound stairs again, do you blame me? I often wondered why that gentleman was there, and if he was the reason that the stairs were out of bounds? Who knows?

CHAPTER 4

Why Dolly
I started writing this book in 1987, since then not one word has been written until this week the 8th May 1990. When suddenly Doris Stokes name came into my mind, and knowing my mind I asked why? Although I never knew Doris personally, her life, and brilliant evidence of spirit survival demonstrations are world known, everyone in all walks of life as heard of her, I am sure, and her wonderful gift of mediumship, such a special lady.

I questioned why Doris had come into my mind, always questioning that's me! All the ifs, buts, and whys? The spirit people must get proper fed up with me at times

As I was thinking of Doris a thought came flooding back of one of her books that someone had left with me, it took me hours to find the book I wanted and my patience was wearing thin, I was all hot and bothered, I eventually found it amongst a pile of old papers and books that we had stashed in an old wall unit, there were so many objects of interest in there, (most of the stuff I had forgotten we had) that I almost forgot why I had been searching in the first place. By the time the book I was looking for was found, Tony had arrived home from work after twelve long hours on shift work, sniffing as he came in the door, going yum, yum! Something smells nice? Oopps! Dinners just on its way, your slippers are warmed, and the newspaper is by your chair kiss! Kissy! I had forgotten the time and got side-tracked by finding all our memorabilia that's the story of my life so it was a quick omelette, fruit yogurt and a big grumble from Tony, no not really!

On picking up the book again it still puzzled me why thoughts of Doris had come into my mind. I shall indulge in a little digression here and comment that I met John Stokes, Doris's husband, what a lovely modest man he was! When I eventually opened the book that Doris had written I realized that this was her last book!, and on the inside cover it was stated that she had passed to the spirit world on the 8th May 1987. Also reading those words reminded me of a Spiritualist church that I used to visit in Chatham, Kent and a certain gentleman that used to call me Dolly, I often asked him "why Dolly" and he always said one day you will know!

That was three years ago, and here I was the 8th May I decided to start with my writings again could it be Doris Stokes herself trying to inspire me to get it finished?

Doris, I do feel your presence pushing me on as the pen moves across the paper, also please forgive me, because although your book was left in our home I never did get around to reading about you and your wonderful mediumship, I do now know why your book was left behind by one of our visitors, thank you my dear friend.

CHAPTER 5

Why we ran

Another time and happening I remember so well was again shared with my Mum, it was during the cold, dark early hours of the morning when I suddenly awoke from a deep sleep, petrified at what had appeared in the room, full of fear. I shook Mum so hard and with such conviction she also awoke with quite a start, without either of us saying a word we scrambled out of bed as quickly as we could, and ran for dear life out of the room as fast as our legs would carry us, we ran in complete darkness along the hall and straight into the kitchen where I knocked myself very badly on an electric fire ouch!

Not stopping for anything, even my injury we continued to run, half groping and half stumbling in the dark, on we went through the scullery to the back door and out into the damp cold night air, were we mad or what?

When we had both caught our breath, Mum came to the realisation that we were both standing in the middle of the garden, in the early hours of the morning dressed in nothing but our nightclothes.

Rubbing her eyes in the hope that she would soon awaken from a dream, she asked me, "Ann why were we running?" standing bare-footed on the cold dewy grass and in the dimness of the night I proceeded to tell her that a great big spider was in the bedroom "massive with great big hairy legs" that seemed to stretch out all over the room I exclaimed, holding out my arms as wide as they would go in a bid to describe its enormity.

Our seriousness then dropped away simultaneously and we both just stood there and laughed and laughed.

We then went back inside and Mum bathed my injured leg and put a dressing on it, you know I still have the splintered crack on my shin all these years later, together with a few others picked up along the way, I'll show you if you wish.

When about seven or eight years of age, it was about this time that Mum took me to my first Spiritualist church in Wembley the meetings were held over an hair dresser in Wembley High Street, my natural spiritual instincts became even more heightened my development of a different kind and awareness started to unfold, we sat and joined many meetings of mediumship, it was at this very church at the age of seventeen that I first went up on the rostrum and gave messages of spirit evidence.

Being a natural born child medium it certainly has had its hic-cups and heart-ache I can assure you, as Mum and others have stated our lives are mapped out before we are born, with all the heartache and suffering and the good times as well. Should we believe we bring a lot of pain from our past lives into this life and that it unfolds as it is written? Are we all of spirit, and is life forever? I for one truly believe that it is so, what do you think?

Look under your pillow
On the same subject, I wish to tell you about another spider incident, which happened quite a few years ago, as already mention these crawlies always seem to find me and this occasion was no exception, could it be that them creepy crawlies, and I have Karma to settle?

Going back to when I was a young child, this particular morning, Mum called out to wake me for school it was about 7.30am, or maybe earlier as it was still quite dark, I was still a bit drowsy, suddenly my eyes were wide open! I had noticed an unwanted companion (arrrgh!) staring at me from the wall, normally I would wait for Mum to call me a couple of times, not this time! I was up, and out of bed like a flash, running, which does seem to be the story of my life concerning spiders!

Thinking back to that young age, I always seemed to be tired (yawn!!) no matter how much sleep I had, which is unusual as most children seem to wake up early. Generally speaking there is no such thing as a lie-in (sigh!), as I was to learn much later on in my life having two daughters of my own, their spiritual experiences are certainly another story!

Later on after "Teacher Chang" had well and truly settled into my life as companion, friend, and most importantly a teacher of spiritual philosophy, he has taught me so much, the first lessons were how to switch off that little light, close myself down! "For you my little one" he would say "need your sleep, and health in order for spirit to communicate through you," these words have been repeated many, many times, together with many hard lessons I have had to learn myself, all because I didn't listen to my good friend "Changs" wise words!

Getting back to what I was telling you, whilst eating my porridge (yum! yum! which, by the way I still enjoy). Mum went to remove the you-know-what, she even brought my clothes out to the kitchen for me to get dressed, then off to school I went, and never gave Mr Spider another thought!

I had a nice enough day at school, and even managed to eat most of my school dinner, including lumpy mashed potatoes (yuk!) I arrived home to have my tea of jam sandwiches, and listen to "Flash Gordon" then it was off to bed, say my prayers, and then sleep!

Now here is something I had never done before, and only because "Changs" voice clearly said "Look under your pillow!" The advice was given, and received loud, and clear! There it was! Waiting for me, to go to sleep, before making its rounds, walking over my face with those horrible long hairy legs, sipping at the moisture on my lips, (slurp!) The very thought doesn't bear thinking about, even now.

As you can imagine, the whole street must have been disturbed by my blood curdling screams! Mum was there like a shot! Wandering what all the fuss was about? Then she saw my face, drained of all blood! I was at the same time holding down the pillow, for all I was worth, "what's the problem?" Mum asked, I remember mumbling incoherently, s-spider, spider, under my p-p-pillow,"ah!" She said that is probably the one that got away this morning, it fell down onto the floor or bed, and scampered before I could catch it!

If Mum had told me that, I would have never, ever have slept in the box room ever again!

Moving cautiously away to a safe distance I watched, as Mum picked up the spider (monster!) and put it out of the window, which was rapidly closed, yes!

Many years later I was to discover why spiders and I, never seem to get along, although saying that, I don't mind spiders in the garden so much!

I must add here, my many heart felt thanks to "Chang" and all spirit people that guide and watch over me! Words just don't seem enough, to show my appreciation!

Spiders (Yugs!)

Are you wondering about the boiler, remember the one that Mum had bought second-hand? Especially for boiling up water for bath nights, those horrible scrubbing, pongy soap nights.

I remember when it was delivered, I offered to give our second hand boiler a good clean up, a bit of spit and polish, and as I removed the blue lid there sitting at the bottom was (gulp) the biggest, fattest spider that I had ever seen in my life, monster, and as if this wasn't bad enough he was just a foretaste of other beasts to come later! Arrrgh!

However, this one had spread itself right across the bottom of our boiler, but guess what? Luckily for me it was as dead as a door-nail!

I have always had a phobia about spiders, as you would have guessed, my hands never, ever, went near that boiler again! Forget the spit and polish, all Mum saw was my backside going out the door as quick as lightening, running like a crazy child, yes! from a dead spider, and a mummified one at that. Thank God!

I don't suffer so much these days, because after a little phone call to the council, a man comes around in his pest control van, (happy days) and exterminates all unwanted creepy crawlies, and it doesn't bother me in the slightest that all my neighbours can see the words "Pest Control" emblazoned across the side!

But be rest assured the chemicals they use only deter them spiders, and sends them on their way. I don't care where! It also helps to keep the cats fleas (hop, hop,) at bay. Poor Tony he always knows when hoppers are about, they seem to like his skin, nip,nip, (ouch) they don't bother me though, maybe my skin is like old leather to them?

One particular night that stays with me, as you will see! I went to bed at about 1.00am zzzzzzzzzzzzz. I woke up in the early hours, and needed to use the toilet, which is unusual for me, because when I sleep, it has been said I die! and I never, ever want to use the toilet in the middle of the night, the warning signals must have been there, but as I was still half asleep the signals went unnoticed!

Our bathroom and toilet were situated on the ground floor, right at the back of the house, so off I went down the stairs, through the lounge/diner, and into the kitchen (hello! pussy cats) I just about managed to hold it after such a long trek, phew, as I settled down to do my business, still only half awake,yawn, yawn, can you imagine my surprise when there IT was right beside me on the wall. Mr Spider, it wasn't a very big one, about an inch and a half long including its legs (yuk,) my first thought was to get out of there quickly, and go and wake Tony (my own personal exterminator, he would help send it to the light) never mind him being on an early shift, selfish? Yes and also petrified.

I did manage to finish what I was doing, and no! I didn't wake Tony! I sat in the kitchen, and made a nice cup of sweet tea, and asked spirit to draw close, and to give me Dutch courage if nothing else, all this time I was keeping a watchful eye on the intruder, it wasn't making a move, was it pretending to be asleep? It wasn't fooling me!

After drinking my tea, I picked up the dust pan and brush, and thought "just a little knock on the head, and it's off to spirit life you go my hairy friend, well down the toilet any way," well that was my plan, but this little blighter had other ideas!

Now I ask you, have you ever given a spider a clout, and it has retaliated, gone for you or the brush in this case. Well that's what happened, gulp. It was coming to me (thanks Chang) that this was definitely not "your ordinary" spider, as you know they have eyes and scramble away when danger lurks!

Not so with this little bugger it was very bold indeed, upon seeing the big monster in my hand (brush), perhaps it should be mention here that Tony and I had just arrived back home from overseas, had it got packed away in our suitcases? Hitching a lift to the UK?

So there I was, brush in hand fighting with this little hairy creature, and to say the least sick with fear, imagine my further surprise when it decided not to budge but stay rigidly glued to the same spot! I am sure it was pretending to be asleep, trying to deter me from the task in hand, crafty manoeuvre, what an intelligent blighter!

But my phobia or sense of danger took over from my compassion, and I gave the monster another wallop, and another, it finally fell to the floor, (hooray, victory) poor thing! I felt very brave and swept the crumpled mass into my dustpan, put it down the sink, and washed the remains away, but not before a thorough examination! You know the legs were very hairy with yellow and brown stripes, and it had a sac filled with "blood" maybe it was one of Count Dracula's? Lets check for fangs.

After such a traumatic ordeal it was a case of making myself another cup of sweet tea, and a biscuit, hours had gone by, and I only had matchsticks to keep my eyes open, Tony came down at 4.45am.

After telling him all about it, he went out into the garden, and looked in the drain, there was the curled up body of the dead spider, he carefully picked it up (kitchen towel), and brought it back indoors for a quick once over, mmmm, this doesn't look like an English spider, he said! We both agreed it was probably foreign. If I had put it down the loo, instead of the sink, Tony wouldn't of been able to see it, and concur with my suspicions, thank you spirit friends for inspiring me!

Although I did not feel/sense my spirit friends around, they were obviously close by and looking after me as always and I thank them, with all my heart, if that creepy crawlie, had gone un-noticed, it may have been poisonous, and bitten one of the family, or even myself (gulp! gulp!)

So, what would we do without our spirit friends? Or our own sixth sense?

A black widow

Well into my married life, my two baby girls, Karen and Marcia, being proper live wires, and naturally psychic, (like mother and grandmother) kept me on my toes!

On this particular occasion, after bathing the girls, (no, not in an old tin bath!) I tucked them into bed, and gave them lots of kisses, and cuddles, which by the way, they both insisted on well into their "teens."

My husband was away working at the time, so after settling the girls down, I watched a bit of television (no, not listening to Flash Gordon on the radio,) it wasn't long before I felt sleepy (yawn,) and went off to bed myself, zzzzzz!

I was awoken during the early hours, no, not to see bright spirit lights, quite the opposite. Not only could the street lights be seen through our very thin curtains, but also the shape of something else! Very slowly making its way up the curtain, instantly I recognised the foreboding silhouette, you guessed it, a creepy crawly!

Lying there frozen with fear, my thought process switched to over drive, was I asleep? And in some kind of horrendous nightmare? But no, I was awake, wide awake, watching this monstrous spider, which had the hairiest, fur like legs and body that I have ever seen in my life! "Black Widow," came to mind, although arachnologists may disagree with my description, I don't care!

Even writing about that night has made my skin crawl making me feel cold all over, horrible!

With my husband away I felt alone and petrified, to say the least, this can't be happening I thought, we live in England! Black widow spiders don't live here, although thinking about that now, hasn't there recently been foreign spiders found in some big supermarkets?

Taking a dozen deep breathes I continued to watch this living nightmare, as it marched up the curtains. Its every movement seemed to be slow and deliberate as if it were stalking its prey (me?) It was like watching a movie in slow motion, only who was the star? And who was the victim? It was as if I was mesmerised, I couldn't take my eyes off this monster, even if I wanted to.

I managed, some how to summon up the strength, and switch on the bed side light, then ever so slowly got out of bed, so I could switch on the big ceiling light, my thoughts turned to my girls, such a potentially dangerous spider. This thing if not killed, could wipe us all out, with one little tiny bite! My daughters were just beginning their lives and must be protected at all cost! Where was everyone? Where was my spirit family, and friends? I needed them all now so much!

Bravely I walked towards the window, perspiration poured from me as I took each trembling step, what was I thinking? Closer now! I saw it walk over the curtain rail, and then slowly walk down the other side as bold as brass, on reaching the window my fingers, actually touching the curtain, just to see if I could get some sort of reaction from it, my eyes had not left this black monster, it was going about its business seemingly unaware of my presence, or was it?

Fraught with worry I just couldn't think what to do? Then a very warm, loving, and welcome voice came, yes it was my good friend "Chang." "We are the light my little one" he said, "do not be afraid" then just like magic, the horrible black creature that had caused me so much anxiety, was gone. Actually disappeared, this was another lesson for me!

There is a dark side to life, such negative forces, thinking back now maybe I was a little tired, and run down, missing my husband! Did I forget to say goodnight to my friends, of the spirit life, or to close. To surround myself, and my family, in fact the whole house with Gods loves and light, whatever you may have thought, consider this! Could it be that we need both negative, and positive energies to counteract the balance in our lives?

This was one incident which taught me much, giving me such a lot of knowledge!

After that terrifying ordeal it was three cups of tea, with lots, and lots of sugar, ahhh, and then a good read of a romantic novel, which fortunately happened to be at hand. it helped me to relax, and take my mind off of the earlier reign of terror, through which the unwanted visitation made me suffer. Since that night, and before getting into bed (no matter how late!) I always scrutinise every nook and cranny in the bedroom, with my little hand held torch! I also look under my pillows, and that of my husbands, I have never ever missed a nights checking, no matter where we have been sleeping, also I always make sure that there is a gap between the bed and wall!

CHAPTER 6

Married life
Married life at first was happy, my husband and I worked as a team, we built up a thriving business, we had a nice home in Winchester, and two lovely baby girls, for some years life was good, then things started to go wrong, and we found that we were incompatible.

It was nobody's fault, just simply one of those things, and maybe we both learnt something from our big mistake!

We eventually parted, and I took the girls back to London, where we stayed with Mum and my stepfather George, who I had completely accepted as my Dad. The two girls were coming up to school age, which took their minds off of all the upheaval and I even managed to get myself a little job.

Once again our lives settled down to a happy routine, our spirit family drew even closer at this time giving us all, much love and encouragement, when needed!

After a couple of years my youngest daughter Marcia, who was eight years old at the time, saw her first spirit person! It was her Aunty Eileen, my sister.

Marcia and Karen

Marcia

Daughter Marcia's Experience
Three family members saw Eileen, the girls and I shared a very large bedroom, which was partitioned off, between ourselves, Mum, and Dad (George), our beds were at arms length apart, it was nice and cosy.

It was about 3.30am one morning, when I awoke to see my sister Eileen walking past the bottom of my bed, and looking at me, her dark hair was loosely tied back, she hadn't grown up and was still that little girl, but somehow looked more mature, if that makes any sense?

I often questioned this (Chang) during my spiritual development, and was taught, that spirit people can come through, and show themselves at what ever age they choose, as they have on many occasions to prove spirit survival.

Now getting back to that night, I lay there watching Eileen, overwhelmed that she should come and visit us, enjoying the moment, when suddenly I heard Marcia's whisper, which made me jump, out of my skin "Mummy who is that little girl?" "What is she doing at the bottom of the bed?" Then in a most indignant manner "and what is she doing in our bedroom?" Questions, questions. (hold up, the phone is ringing as I write about this event). It was Marcia phoning, as if on cue, COINCIDENCE and not for the first time either, thanks to that inventor of BT,ha ha, mind you it could have been spirit intervention, it gave me the opportunity to ask her if she still remembered her first manifestation of spirit, yes she did! After recovering from hearing Marcia's little whisper, which by the way sounded so natural, and matter of fact, we both just laid there and observed Eileen as she disappeared into the curtained closet, which was opposite the end of the girls bunk beds.

Such a quiet moment, as if time stood still, it was as if everything else had been forgotten, this magical time of sharing together, how very honoured we were, such a privilege. Marcia was very quiet indeed, there wasn't a sound! I wanted to ask what was going through her mind? How did she feel? What were her thoughts upon seeing the little girl (my sister, her Aunty Eileen!)

Karen my other daughter was still fast asleep in the top bunk, oblivious to what was going on, then I heard Marcia whisper again "why has that little girl gone into the closet? Is her bed in there?" This shared experience will stay with me, and I feel Marcia forever!

It took what seemed like an age for Marcia to go back to sleep, she was not in the least afraid, but was filled with excitement, and wonderment!

Lying quietly many thoughts were floating in and out of my mind, I kept thinking back to when I first heard Marcia whisper, and I wondered if she would still remember the event in the morning? Which unfortunately for me came to soon. This was Marcia's first spirit materialisation, or had there been others? That she did not mention or understand? Maybe she thought they were her imagination!

Three generations share

In the morning I tried to put the night before out of my mind as best as I could. I busily got the breakfast sorted, and the girls ready for school, all the time I was aching to ask Marcia if she remembered anything from the night before? You will understand that it was important that Marcia mentioned it without prompting from me!

It did seem as though she had forgotten as she did not mentioned anything at all! Then right out of the blue came a voice, not Marcia's, but Mum's! She had been quietly sitting at the table, drinking her tea, listening to the girls chit-chat as they ate their breakfast, Chomp! Chomp she mentioned about the visit from Eileen, "she simply stood quietly beside the bed, and then she turned and walked into your room" then Mum asked "did you see her Ann?" That is the way it has always been with Mum and I, this lovely awareness, how blessed I have been! Now before I had the chance to open my mouth and answer, Marcia chipped in saying, "I saw her too Nanny, she walked into the closet, ah, so Marcia had remembered our little visitor from the night before!

What a fantastic event for all three of us to experience, how privileged we had been, it must be quite unique for three generations of the same family to wake at the same time, and all see the same spirit visitor, my sister Eileen! It was like a family reunion, which I know we will all cherish for ever! I believe that moments like these are a gift from God. Absolutely wonderful!

The following are just a few of the many spiritual experiences that I feel may be of extreme interest to you, both concern our family;

The first I wish to write of, is about our eldest daughter Karen's visual spirit encounter, Karen had by this time married, and started her own little family, her best friend Julie, had just recently passed her driving test (first time) and had bought herself a little car,brum, brum, honk, and was feeling that life was very good, however a terrible tragedy was about to take place, not far from where she lived in Rochester she was involved in a tragic collision with a lorry, at a very busy roundabout, Julie was instantly killed. I visited Karen a few days after this tragic event, whilst we were chatting about Julie, our emotions obviously were still very close to the surface, Corrina our granddaughter was playing with her toys,when Karen suddenly stopped in mid-sentence and almost shouting said "Mum, Julie is overshadowing you!" Not only facially, but my whole mannerism, as soon as I became aware of this transformation. I felt her spirit draw back!

This little event helped, especially Karen come to terms with the loss of her dear friend, to know that she was still close to her and that she had arrived safely spirit-side, where she would continue her own life's progression. All of this time Corrina continued to play happily with her toys!

The second spiritual happening I would like to mention here concerns our granddaughter Corrina who was about 3 years old at the time!

Spirit activity evident in a photograph of Corrina, aged 3

More spirit activity evident in a photograph of Corrina, aged 8

They had two lovely pussy-cats one called Brandy, and the other Shandy. Brandy had gone on a bit of a walk about, and she hadn't come home for a couple of nights, the dirty stop-out!

Karen was beginning to get a bit worried about her and decided to put a notice concerning her cat in the local shop window, at the same time she also put leaflets through people's doors in the street and local neighbourhood.

A lady soon came knocking on her door, saying that she had found a cat in the kerb outside her home! Karen went to see the cat, it was Brandy poor baby, she bought Brandy home, and they buried her in a lovely little plot in the back garden. One day not long after this event, Corrina said to her Mum out of the blue, "Mummy, Brandy is sitting in the window!" Karen had not seen the cat herself, and replied that it was probably Shandy that was in the window. "No" Corrina argued "it was Brandy" I know my cat and what I saw, let me remind you that Corrina was only 3 years old at the time!

How wonderful spirit are, and what fantastic gifts they give to us, allowing us to see them in their spirit body.

We are hoping to place in this book a few special pictures of our Granddaughter Corrina, one taken of her at Xmas, when she was about 3 years old showing a spirit rod and mists beside her, the other was when she was about 8-10yrs old, and taken at an holiday camp there are lots of spirit mist around her, it seems to be the story of our family life, very naturally spirit are drawn to us, as they are to everyone, and indeed show themselves in many shapes and forms.

What about your spirit experiences, I would love to hear from you about them!

Corrina with Karen

CHAPTER 7

There are so many pathways
Life goes on in its own sweet way, or does it? Visiting Spiritualist churches had become a way of life over the years, and no matter where we lived there was always one to be found. Sometimes meetings were held way out in the country, with not even a proper road to go down just a dirt track leading to a little hut in the middle of a field! But then again how nice those times were all like of mind people gathered in small groups discussing, and exchanging points of view, of spirit philosophy, of life ever lasting, as these words are written it would seem that those days are gone! Well I say no, they are here and now, and in the future too, are we walking in circles? What do you think?

Listening and grasping for all knowledge, digesting every word, our development goes on and on we never stop developing, so make sure you do the same, the future of Spiritualism depends on you all it really does!

There are so many pathways, all with lessons for us to learn, some can be very frustrating and the loneliness can at times seem unbearable, but at other times pathways we go down can be so rewarding! the magic of it all sometimes leaves us speechless!

Physical Circle
Share with us yet more spiritual experiences that occurred in my first closed physical circle.

I had been attending a certain church for some time, and one evening after the service, the circle teacher asked me if I would like to join their physical circle, well I have always said "nothing ventured, nothing gained" always in at the deep end that's me! (Sink or swim!) Little did I know then, but it was to be the beginning of many changes to come, both happy and sad.

Arriving at 8.00pm this particular night as instructed, I felt nervous yet excited, crazy or what? Having never sat in this kind of circle before, I really did not know what to expect, (my head was spinning) and this was a closed physical circle, people usually went on waiting lists for years! to get a seat, I was so lucky and privileged to join one so quickly.

There were eight other members including the teacher/control, a man called Robert who seemed very nice. After being introduced to everyone I went to my seat and sat down, I still did not know, or understand physical circle work, or what was involved? Nothing as yet had been explained to me so I was thinking, "is this it?" No argument was coming from "Chang", which made a change!

The main light was switched off, (Hello!) Which left a little red light emitting the tiniest glow, I couldn't see a thing at first, and was waiting for my eyes to adjust! settling right down into my seat feeling nervous and also I don't mind admitting, a little afraid my imagination at that moment was working overtime! I began to wonder what the hell I had let myself in for? Had I come to the wrong meeting? Was I mad? Has this ever happened to you? If so you will definitely know what I felt like!

The control of the group was speaking in a voice that did not sound like his, asking in prayer, for Gods blessing! Well that was a relief (phew!) by this time my feelings were all over the place, then this strange voice was speaking telling us all to quieten ourselves down to the inner self, breath deeply, and softly, comfortably, close our eyes, and still the mind, which was a lot easier said then done! I can tell you!

I closed my eyes, and was waiting for them to stop fluttering around in their sockets; also at the same time, trying to control my physical body from fidgeting, and control my heart that was beating like a time bomb getting ready to explode! I was sure that I must be disturbing the other members of the circle. I then became aware of their breathing, and believe that this helped me to settle, my heart beat began to slow, and I started to relax, my eyes became still, tightly closed as if stuck with super glue (was super glue invented then?). Perhaps they had been closed by unseen hands! I couldn't even slit them open, although believe me I did try, there's nothing worse then not being in control of ones faculties!

As I began to relax, so my breathing became more even, and deeper, well this isn't so bad after all! My awareness then became more heightened then usual, as did my excitement at sensing the etheric energies swirling all about us, thickening and congesting in the air, all those lovely spirit people gathering, drawing close, I could feel them all touching my face, head and hair, they felt like fluffy feathers, making me want to scratch where their touches had been! There was also shimmering sensations down my spine, my whole body was at this point vibrating!

Then came this feeling of being lifted up, as though coming out of my body, there is not really words in the dictionary to describe all that

I was feeling! the noticeable aromas! My body was still lifting up and up out of the chair! Should this be happening? Sit quietly and control your movement is what was said, not to hover above ones chair! Like a monkey, it was an impossible situation, so much happening all at once, never had I felt this way before, never!

I called out to "Chang" whom I had completely forgotten about.(silly me) I then heard his voice shouting, "well you don't have to shout I am not deaf! He wasn't really shouting, it was just that all my senses were extremely heightened, like static electricity at every sound, a high pitched echo in my ears! "Chang" then said "open your eyes my little one I never argue with his commanding voice never! "Take control of this situation, control the spirit within you"

Not so easy of course, and all right for him to say, but my eyes still felt like they were glued together however they did open, after much effort which seemed to take ages, probably only a moment or so!

The musty aroma (ectoplasm) seemed to linger for ages, I truly feel that if I had not opened my eyes my heart may have stopped, thank you dear "Chang" for always being there, what would I do with out you?

On opening my eyes, and adjusting to the light, which "in my absence" had been switched on, I could see all the eyes of the circle staring at me! Had they noticed my predicament? Apparently not, as they all commented on how relaxed and contented I looked, what! That was hard to believe, I thought that they were all being kind as it was my first time, any way I kept everything to myself, "Chang" agreed that this was wise, explaining that it was my spirit body (levitating).

That was the beginning of many weeks, months, and years to follow, sitting for development of physical mediumship, it sure had its moments. There were so many strange experiences! Some nice, some not so nice! Although all very enlightening and as you know patience is a virtue, something we all need to control!

The bonds that we made sharing those evenings were so strong and fruitful, that we became like a family, all young sensitives together, nice don't you think? That time will never be forgotten, but it was time for me to move on, as the teacher had asked me to give up my seat, saying that other doors were about to open up to me! How right he was.

Sitting in that circle also gave us all the opportunity to meet other mediums, to talk and listen to their experiences.

Each Sunday one of us, depending on whose name was on the rota, played host to the medium that was taking the service, what great fun that was, we would make tea or coffee, and little sandwiches, and although life takes us in many different directions, and yes through many open doors, times like those stay in our hearts always!

It was around this time that I was invited to a fledglings evening mind you I didn't realise that it would mean going onto the platform (ouch!) talk about being thrown in at the deep end, story of my life!

What was I supposed to do once up there, give messages/clairvoyance? somebody must have thought so, could it possibly have been "Chang", thanks friend, till now one to one readings, and speaking with my spirit friends and family was my limitation, this was going to be a very new experience,would my mouth even open?

Walking towards that platform (rostrum) with my legs feeling like wobbly jelly, thinking that at any moment I am going to pass out, (thud! No not a spirit rap, that's my body hitting the floor!)...my stomach was upside down, and I was s-s-shaking like I had DTs, my eyes felt as though they were popping right out of my head, was this what a nervous breakdown felt like? Would I suddenly wake up in a straight jacket laughing to myself? Ha! Ha! Maybe so! Is this how all up and coming young sensitives felt? Or was it just me?

After what seemed like ages I found myself up on the rostrum, facing a sea of faces! (Gulp!) trying now, to avoid making eye contact with anyone!... but everywhere I turned there were eyes looking at me in anticipation, penetrating my very being! I managed to stutter out a small opening prayer, the only bit I can recall now is A-A-Amen!

Praying also in my head to the spirit life for guidance, for Gods love, time now to open my mouth, mumbling sounds coming out!

Then nothingness, only light and mists, and spirit people all around what sheer bliss, I could have stayed there forever, everything else before this moment forgotten, eventually coming out of this wonderful state, to the realization that I was standing on the rostrum to hear deafening sounds of people clapping? I immediately turned to see who had stepped up onto the rostrum, no-one, oh! They must be clapping me! Feeling a little self-conscious, stiff, and freezing cold,brrrr. Is this what service to spirit meant? Rostrum work? If so "Must go back to the drawing board, couldn't put body through this again, never!" Crikey! how all those mediums I had seen must suffer, to serve man and spirit!

Then I heard "Chang's" voice saying, "This is the pathway that you have come to serve my little one, congratulations!"

I was now stepping off the rostrum, walking back to my seat, still feeling unwell, not myself at all and what about messages? Had there been any given? It wasn't until later whilst having a very, much needed sweet cup of tea, and a handful of yummy biscuits, that people came up to thank me for the messages, and, to confirm the evidence that came through with such tremendous love, wow! Magic! Delighted, overjoyed, and floating on air, that was how I felt for many weeks following that particular evening as pleased as I felt, I never forgot to thank my dear friend and companion "Chang" and all family, friends, spirit, for without them none of it would ever have been possible, we walk together always! All their patience, time and most of all love, they never fail us ...never!... always there to give little pushes, giving strength, and courage helping us to move on at the right times, also there to give praise where it is due!... and sometimes help dry our tears! They truly show us by their deeds that they come in Gods light!

That evening brought about changes, that took me into many different areas of Spiritualism, all helping with my growth and understanding, which at this point was still very limited! Had I so far learned so very little? It comes to my mind whilst writing these words, that I for one have only just touched upon "True life" spirit knowledge is, as it seems limitless, and we on earth have but scratched the surface!

Looking back now to that fledglings evening, I can see that it was the start of a very heart warming way of life for me, little old me serving as a medium, who would have thought that? Mind you my hair has now turned grey, (no not highlights!) and my physical body (sob!) is starting to crumble and the stress, well we won't go into that! Unless you have a year to spare! Mind you if I could turn back the clock, I really don't think that I would change a thing!

CHAPTER 8

Tony came into our lives

The girls were growing up fast and it was nice to watch their individual personality's blossom, and unfold. Of course their human development had its moments, but on the whole life was very good, and we were happy.

After giving up my seat in Robert's circle, with him informing me that other doors would soon be opening to me, I was invited to join another closed circle, to share and assist David the circle teacher/control.

Not one day had passed by without me sitting for meditation, for at least ten minutes per day, which is most beneficial to ones personal and spiritual growth, at around this time we decided to open our own home for discussion/meditation circles. Those evenings were like magic all of us learning and understanding wisdom, that came through from the spirit life, sometimes we stayed up talking well into the early hours, yawn! yawn! Such happiness and laughter shared, as well as many cups of tea (slurp!) and yummy! Biscuits.

Humbly we serve spirit, to the best of our ability, always hoping that some of those that attended, might one day go out onto their own pathways to help and serve others, spreading out like ripples in a pond!!

Life became very hectic, being a lone parent family and serving many Spiritualist churches/centres. There never seemed to be enough hours in the day or energy, and some times I literally crawled into my bed, and slipped into a coma like sleep zzzzzzzzz!

I was every now and again, awaken for no apparent reason? Bet you can guess who it was? Yep! Spirit people! It was about this time I think that I first used one of my favourite expression. "Bugger off, I need my sleep" very articulate don't you think?

More lessons to learn I know, but you do have to stress to spirit people sometimes that your physical body needs its rest, it took ages before an agreement was reached, so frustrating it made me feel like pulling my hair out, if I did I would have begun to resemble "Kojak".

So many lessons for us to learn, grow together, in harmony can this be the only way forward, in my opinion you and spirit have got to become as one, yet still retain that individual spark!

It was about this time that Tony came into our lives, (no he didn't just turn up one day on the door step,) mind you that would have been something to write about don't you think? And this was to be the man although not knowing it at the time, to spend the following years of our lives with, which reminds me "Mr Hungry" will be home for his dinner soon, going off now to prepare food, don't go away, I will be back!

Yum! Yum! Very nice dinner one of our favourites lamb chops and veg with gravy, and mint sauce. Tony now settled in his chair, cat (sunny) on his lap, newspaper in his hand (page three!) I bet I couldn't count to ten before he drops off for a little snooze 1, 2, zzzzzzzz! Told ya!

Left, Tony and me 30 years ago and, below, now

Getting back to Tony and those early days, he moved in lock stock and barrel as the saying goes, into our lives, love and hearts with no time wasted, he swept us clean off our feet (phew!), all within a matter of weeks with not even the tinniest utterance of argument from either my daughters or myself, it all happened so naturally, although there was one big hic-cup as far as Spiritualism was concerned he was sceptical, probably frightened of the unknown

We all manage to fit into a nice routine living together as a family, the girls took to Tony with big hearts, although there were a few teething problems, but that happens in any family. I had been told that changes were coming (Tony?) and as they say nothing ventured nothing gained, surely this is the very essence of life itself, how can we hope to grow without change?

Looking back to those years I often thought, poor Tony, what had he let himself in for, a ready made family is one thing but one that believed in the dead living on for ever was entirely a different matter!

What fun the spirit people had welcoming him into our lives they would give him a little touch here, (who's that?) and a little tickle there, and cold breezes down his spine, making his hair stand on end, like a punk rocker! Spirit are naughty aren't they? Ha! Ha! But then he had joined a family of natural psychics, what do you expect? The thought was sent out please help Tony with his scepticism and fear of spirit, and to watch his gradual acceptance of spirit was truly a wonderful event, and very uplifting.

Most happenings would occur when Tony was at home with the girls, while I was out serving Spiritualist churches, the girls being used to such happenings hardly noticed anything, I say again poor Tony, his eyes were certainly being opened! Its not nice being thrown in at the deep end, or in his case diving in and although Tony is a strong swimmer, this time he was against the current! Glug! Glug! Mr Fish! I did wonder at the time if maybe it was all getting too much for him, I didn't want the spirit people to drive him out the door, one minute I must have a cuppa my throat gets very dry when I'm writing, I think its got something to do with the fact that I actually say the words as I write them sometime I wonder why I bother to write at all, because as soon as I have written about 50 words I usually feel like a little snooze! I wonder if other writers suffer from these conditions, by the way I did enjoy my cup of tea and little cakes yum! yum!

All of my life I have trusted spirit implicitly so I knew that what ever they had in store for Tony he would be able to cope, I felt very strongly that they had plans for us, and knew within my heart that he would soon receive the spirit proof that would change his sceptical outlook!

However I was a bit concerned, but my hands were tied, "Chang" had advised me to keep a low profile, (well I am only 5ft 2in) from the beginning Tony refused point blank to discuss this Spiritualism mumbo! Jumbo! Mediumship! I had learnt from a very young age to respect other people's feelings! "Be patient, my little one" Chang would whisper.

We were so happy apart from that one little hic-cup; I would often stay awake at night worrying about him! Could he as spirit had said, be able to live with this family of psychics, we were a close family apart from the spiritual aspect, the girls even had pet names for Tony (not all printable.) One is da da which our youngest Marcia still uses even today. Sometime later he started to take me to Spiritualist churches, and stood outside while I took the service (dummy,) waiting to take me home afterwards, it was extremely hard to keep a low profile as "Chang" had advised! It was well worth the wait!! As you will read later, gradually, slowly curiosity was getting the better of him, and he began to ask me little probing questions, only tiny ones but the door was beginning to open! Then we began to have little discussions. (Halleluiah!) Someone had switched a light on, thank you spirit, and my good friend "Chang" for all your hard work.

Tony's first materialisation sketch with a photograph of Fred's grandfather for comparison

74

Then one day out of the blue Tony said that he would like to be part of the congregation, "just to see what it was all about", it was so nice seeing him sitting at the back of the church, nearest the door I was taking the service so it was a bit of an eye opener for him you could say, after that time I had trouble shutting him up! Questions, questions he sometimes disturbed my sleep, which is not something that is recommended. The difference was noticeable, this was the real Tony the inner him words cannot express how we both felt at that time. His understanding and quick mind, grasped at knowledge, it was truly fun watching all the fear and doubt disappear from him it was as if all his birthdays had come at once, I am sure that if he didn't have two left feet he would have danced around with excitement.

We always found time to sit (meditation) every day to further his progression, Tony was invited into our development home circles, but always declined our invitations saying that he was more then happy to sit with just me and him we were growing spiritually closer all the time, although there were big tests to come!

Before I write about this special event, I wonder if my own doubts and worries were more test lessons for me to learn, I think they probably were, what do you think?

Tony's first materialization
We were living in Rochester at the time, and had earlier this particular day bought a piece of furniture, that came in three heavy parts. It was an extremely hot day, well up into the high seventies or eighties (phew!) I don't know what was worse the heat or the weight of the furniture parts; he was huffing and puffing like an old bull after carrying in two pieces from the boot of the car which was parked at the kerb, he would not let me help him, as I was a little frail at the time, poor me!

Suddenly I heard Tony gasp and drop the last piece of furniture, down it went with a crash, oh no, I thought, or something similar, on going outside to see what the matter was, Tony was mumbling to me something about a man, what man? I couldn't see anyone! had someone come and tripped him over making him drop the furniture? Is that what he was trying to say?

After a few moments, once he had composed himself he explained that he was lifting the last piece of furniture out of the boot when this man appeared saying "come on lad you can do it, last piece now!" and with a big beaming smile he was gone, vanished, de-materialized.

At the same time as Tony was telling me what had happened, he was drawing this person's face on a piece of paper, and explaining to me what this man was wearing right down to the colour of his eyes and the suit that he wore it is difficult to describe Tony's excitement, as he had not only met a spirit person but was also drawing his portrait, this was the first time that I had seen him draw anything. Apparently he used to draw as a child but had not done so for many years, and this was the first time that he had actually seen or heard a spirit person in his life. Could this be a gift that the spirit world had given to him? Had it lain dormant, until triggered by this event? I for one believe that this is so!

From that day to this he has certainly put his special artistic gifts to work for the spirit world, drawing many spirit people for their family and friends, we now serve side by side (dream come true!) in the Spiritualist churches/centres.

He still to this day has that scrap of paper with the spirit mans face sketched on it, as I write he draws close to me "Hello friend" thank you for showing yourself to Tony, and thank you for allowing me to write about that special event.

Fred's grandfather, left and above, our house in Rochester

20th November 2006

As you will know, having read this book so far it has been sitting on the self collecting dust, once again since 1990, or there abouts!

However a certain gentleman! Yes, you guessed it! my good friend "Chang" has recently been whispering in my ear. Nag! Nag! Nag! Write! Write! Write! "It may have past your attention my little one" he said, using his pet name for me, "So sorry to mention this, but now that you are in your 63rd year, and a pensioner, you are getting a weeny bit forgetful," you cheeky!

So to recap I was telling you all about Tony, and his wonderful gift of psychic-art, or spirit-art as he likes to call it!

Since he first saw the gentleman by the kerb, outside our house in Rochester, remember when he was moving that last piece of furniture from the boot of the car huffing and puffing like an old bull in the heat of the day, and it really was a hot day phew! That really was such a magical time, he was as excited as a baby that's just had its first birthday party and thinking about it now spiritually, he was just a baby taking his first steps! No I didn't feed him rusks!

You are probably thinking, is Ann loosing it? She seems to be repeating words that she has already written, let me explain, I have found it extremely difficult to commence writing this book again, its been nearly 20yrs since I last put pen to paper (apart from Tesco's shopping lists) it feels like I'm learning to ride a bike all over again. I'm sure that some of you know what that feels like!

So please don't get bored, you will be amazed at Tony's spiritual life, and development I promise you wont be disappointed!

That first ever spirit portrait, by the way has sat in a folder of precious kept spiritual membrobillia along beside an actual photograph, of the very gentleman that appeared to Tony!

The Sawing noises

Writing about Tony's extremely spiritual event, reminds me of another! A very noisy spirit person indeed, clank! Clank!

We had not long moved to Rochester and into a very yuppy, three up and down maisonette, we settled in nicely and got to know the neighbours, now bear with me here, as I step back in time once again to some years ago, don't be confused, this is an experience with a difference!

It sounded like some-one sawing, and we wondered if it was one of the neighbours, it always occurred late at night or in the early hours of the morning, some-one was being very inconsiderate!

We discovered on enquiring to the other residents, that they had also heard this inconsiderate person sawing at odd hours! But no-one could trace the source of the disturbance!

Following this odd event, we found that our taps were being turned on at night when we were all tucked up in our beds, going off into a state of unconsciousness zzzzzzzzz! It was always the cold tap never the hot one! Thank God, as this would have run up a big bill, then the central heating started to come on, and stay on Hot! Hot! Hot! We thought at first, it could be the girls, playing a joke on us having a right laugh,.but we soon ruled that possibility out, as the heating would come on when they were at school, or sound asleep, late at night! We had the boiler and time switch checked by an engineer, to make sure that there was nothing electrically wrong with the system, nothing was found wrong, all working perfectly!

This carry-on coincided with the early days of Tony's development, when he was still very sceptical, but he couldn't logically dismiss things that were going on around us, some of which he had witnessed first hand, he wasn't to happy, and neither were the girls and I, as we were all getting bags under our eyes, through lack of undisturbed sleep! Rumour had it that when the maisonettes were being built, a carpenter/jack of all trades, had fallen from the scaffolding, (poor! poor! man), and had died almost instantaneously, although only a rumour it did seem to make sense to all those that knew about it!

A neighbour that lived just a couple of doors away, told us that she always felt a strange presences when walking up her stairs, woooo! although she stressed that she was not afraid, quite the opposite really she always felt (being a one parent family) that she was being looked after, it made her "feel secure" her very words.

This particular lady moved to be nearer her daughter's school, and when we used to bumped into her, have a little natter/gas-bag she would always express her regret that she had moved, as she missed, as she put it her guardian angel! We felt strongly that this was the same person/ carpenter that had fallen off the scaffolding, maybe he was having problems, not realising he was in fact dead of the physical body, and was still going about his building work! What do you think?

We ourselves have long since moved from those maisonettes, and I often wonder if those strange events are still being witnessed to-day nearly 30 yrs later.

CHAPTER 9

The Organ

Fred Mattman, a good friend, colleague, a great Spiritualist medium, and speaker, who we have known for more years then we care to remember, was telling us that his daughter had just bought, a new Yamaha organ, and asked us if we would like the old one, as she was a bit cramped for space, as you can imagine being an older organ it was big, and very grand in all its glory!

"Yes" we said, and Fred promptly delivered it to us! We made room for it in our lounge, right in front of our back window that looked out into the garden. I remember it so well standing there tall and proud, its lovely dark wood, sun-light reflecting off its polished surfaces all through the seasons.

When Mum, who, came from an extremely gifted musical family used to visit us she would always be plonk, plonking, away on it to her hearts content, she was in her element, (eat your heart out Liberace!) Although I can't say the same for our neighbours! Keep this to yourself, but Tony and I needed earplugs! As Mum was now in her older age, her best playing days were certainly behind her, just a little off key, sorry Mum!

The organ was with us for about eight years, before it one day decided it had had enough, and expired on us, very sad! So there it stood (collecting dust) in all its glory, in front of the window enjoying the view, and the sunshine.

The cats – Tabs, Ayesha and Sunny with our special organ

Could we have it repaired? Could we afford it? Yes! of course we could, well maybe, if it doesn't cost to much! So it was out with the yellow pages, and after many phone calls we managed to find an organ repairer, by the name of Fred, who coincidently lived just around the corner, literally, two minutes away, from us (spirit at work again?) We made an appointment for him to come to our house, and when he arrived he bought along his partner, another coincidence was that we all knew each other, as Fred played his lovely organ music at many of the Spiritualist churches that we served! Now as "Chang" commented earlier I must be getting old and forgetful, because for the life of me, I can't recall his partners name, I must eat more grapes as they are supposed to be good for brain damage!

What a very special day that turned out to be, the most amazing, dumb founded conversation took place, during which time we had numerous cups of tea, and biscuits (for sugar drops that we all seemed to suffer!), and sandwiches to stave off starvation, as our conversations went way past mid-night! Fred it turn out had lived in our house as a boy, with his parents and grand-parents.

Our house, our lovely home, that we had only moved into a few months earlier, are you picking up mentally, what I am about to write? That gentleman that appeared to Tony when he was struggling with the furniture, was in fact "Fred's" Grand-father! Wow!

Fred's Grandfather

Words can not express the look of delight, and shock on his face, when we showed him the childlike portrait that Tony had drawn, he confirmed that it was indeed a likeness of his grand-father, and even went back to his home to fetch loads of photographs, one of which he let us have, and we have kept it safe ever since, as Fred walked around our house, he knew every nook and cranny, and explained to us, all the alterations that had been made since he lived there! And the fact that he used to sleep in the cellar "That was my bedroom" he said, big smile on his face, he told us many stories of his lovely memories!

From the moment we first viewed our house, we felt a pull towards it, and the day we moved in, felt to us like we had come home! There was always a warm feeling to the house, that was not only felt by us, but was noticed by our friends, and family members, we lived for many happy years in that lovely house, with Fred's spirit family, and those loving warm conditions that were impregnated into the walls, we always knew that we were being looked after.

By the way the organ was never repaired; apparently it had completed its life span.. (sigh, sniff,) so very sad! Fred came around, and took the poor thing away, to his home, and broke it up for spares, no more plonk! plonking, for Mum. You never know some other organ may have received a transplant from our old organ, which would mean parts of it might be still be going strong, nice thought isn't it!

Spirit Cat Lady

We constructed a lean-to at the side of the house, outside our back kitchen door, not long after we had moved in; it was only made of plastic with an aluminium frame. We found many uses for it over the years our tumble dryer lived happily in it, and our seeds, potted plants, and cuttings all thrived in there over the winter giving us lovely displays through out the seasons.

It was while washing up, that I first saw her, out of the kitchen window this lovely spirit lady! She would either be walking into the lean-to or out towards the garden. The cats would often look out towards the lean-to, and I am sure that they could see her, meow, meow, or maybe she was giving them all an occasional little stroke, I feel sure that she was a catty person, like ourselves.

It was lovely sitting out in the kitchen, eating yummys, and having little glimpses of her, she might have even taken it into her head to pot up a few plants for us ... can't say we ever noticed, we did notice the lovely feelings and scented aroma, that always accompanied her visits.

Lilly's Photo

We have always taken lots of photographs, and make a point, once we have had them developed, of checking for any "extras" like a little spirit rod, a spirit face or anything else that can't be easily explained!

One photograph that comes to mind is of our little Devon-Rex pussycat named "Lilly" this particular picture was taken of her as she sat on the kitchen window seal; she was a very pretty girl, meow, meow, and being a little conceited, loved to have her picture taken! I had loaded the camera and then it was snap! Snap! Snap! Gotcha! Normally she would move at the last moment, and the pictures would come out slightly blurred, as we all know animals can be unpredictable, the only time she was still was when she was sleeping zzzzzzz! Even then she would jump about twitching all over the place, you could see that she was definitely dreaming.

After we had this batch developed, there was one that stood out like a sore thumb; it was so very different from the rest, it was the one of "Lilly" in the window, it came out coloured lilac and purple, very unusual! There was also some tiny balls of light in the back ground, could be reflections? or maybe they're spirit lights? We like to think that perhaps it was the spirit lady trying to show herself, you can judge for yourself if I can find that photo! I will put it in this book for all to share!

The spirit lady (Catty lady as we nick named her) stayed with us until we moved some years later, and what with "Fred's" grandfather out the front of the house, we felt, as did those who visited us that we were being well and truly looked after by spirit.

Our little Devon Rex, Lilly

Hurricane in 1987
Do you remember when we had the hurricane in 1987; Tony has just reminded me that it was a Wednesday? anyway our street was wrecked, fences and roof tiles were blown off and scattered all up the road, windows were smashed in, trees uprooted, it was horrendous! But we never even lost a roof tile, spirit looking after us? Also the chicken wire fence that we put up, to stop Max our Doberman,bark, bark, from taking a dip in the fish pond or romping in the flower beds stayed up, and firmly in place never moved an inch!

Tony was working a night-shift that particular night, when he left home at 9.15pm it was very windy, we had been assured by Michael Fish the TV weather man, that any strong winds were going to "Die Out" before they reached us, some-one was telling porkies!

At about 3am the bedside phone rang, waking me up, with a bit of a start from the deepest sleep! Max who slept on a cushion beside the bed gave me a disgruntled look as though the phone ringing was somehow my fault, and then pushed his nose back under his cover, lazy bones, I reached out and turned on the bedside lamp, nothing? Great, the bulb must have blown, being a little concerned now who could be ringing me at this time? I managed to locate the phone in the dark, hellooo, it was "Tony" he was excited, although he was trying to speak calmly. "Go down stairs" he said, I was still only half awake and wasn't sure if this was some kind of dodgy call? If I had my little yellow whistle to hand I would have blown it down the phone! "Go down stairs" he said again "I'll be home soon" my mind started to clear as I replaced the receiver, what was that howling noise, and the crashing sounds coming from outside? Stumbling out of bed in the dark to the window I could see lots of debris flying through the air, blimey! I truthfully was not afraid for myself! my main concern was for "Tony" as I am sure he said he was on his way home, how could he be driving in this weather? and with all this rubbish strewn across the road?

I put my slippers, and dressing gown on, Max was there at my side staring up at me with a worried look on his face, trying to work out if his Mum was once again sleep walking, woof, woof! He must have walked miles with me over the years during my little night time excursions!

We carefully went down stairs, the cats were already awake to greet us, I scrambled around in the kitchen drawers, where did I put the candles? After a short while I managed to find them and had just lit one up when out of the front window I saw "Tony" in a state of shock! Pulling up at the kerb, there was rubbish and tree branches all over the car (Capri).

Thank God we had a gas cooker, as you will remember, all the electricity was off and Tony had to leave work without having a shower, he was like a coal-miner as black as soot! as he worked in a foundry…I had to boil loads of saucepans of water to fill up the bath, it reminded me of the war days, we laughed so much, I wouldn't have recognised him if it wasn't for his Bristol accent. The bath was followed by lots of tea and toast, yummy!

As we sat in the kitchen talking Tony told me that the roof covering the foundry where he worked (Kent Alloys) casting wheels, had been ripped off by the wind and as it was made of toughened glass, it shattered, covering the floor, even the metal roof struts started to bend, there were a few cuts and bruises but luckily most of the men like Tony managed to get out of the way before anyone suffered serious harm, he described it to me as looking like something during the blitz, not that he was born then, ha, ha, the drive home, although only ten minutes was just as hazardous as trees were coming down as he drove by blocking his way, the roads were covered in rubbish, and glass, he also mentioned that the front of the car kept trying to go up, and the fact that the wind kept pushing the car backward, he was to scared to take it out of second gear, 20mph max! I can't think how he managed to control the car in the heart of the hurricane? But here he was safe and sound to tell the tale, the reason that he had phoned, and asked me to go down stairs was because our house was about 120yrs old, and even mild winds had been known to blow the old chimney stacks down, (gulp) and our chimney was situated right above our bedroom! Although he must have had lots of things on his mind, his first thought was "Call Ann" actually I have never thought to ask him where he phoned from? We never had mobiles back then, just asked him and he said that there was a pay phone by the main gate.

Our neighbours Simon and Allison did suffer some damage to their chimney; although it didn't fall down, they did loose quite a few bricks from around the base making it very unsafe!! It was leaning towards the rear of our house, and "Thank God" it didn't fall, because if it had it would have crashed down into our kitchen area where our (babies!) cats slept in their catty house, meow, meow, ouch!

Our neighbour on the other side, Maureen, and her two little girls came into us at about 6.30am for breakfast and a wash and brush up, as their house was all electric. The whole situation was very unreal a bit like a dream, a very bad dream! Extremely frightening for her little girls. We nattered for awhile about the hurricane the loudness of it all, and the damage that it had caused.

Group room yellow carpet
We decided to convert our little back bedroom into a special Group-room, where we could hold spiritual evenings, discussion groups, and development circles, for those of a like mind. We painted the walls a pale sky blue, and lilac colour, then we went out and bought a second-hand three piece which was brown, with a yellow flower pattern on it. The only thing that remained to do was the floor covering, if we could get a

nice yellow carpet, that would be just about right, it would really enhance the furniture, to be honest here, we were thinking at the time "there's no chance" its not every day that you see a yellow carpet for sale, (not a very fashionable colour) especially not the shade we wanted, so it was decided that blue carpet would have to do, mind you I still sent the thought out to spirit, as they say "nothing ventured nothing gained!

We were still busy decorating the rest of the house, and sorting out all the bric-a-brac that we had accumulated over the years, which meant several trip to the local council tip. You know it is utterly amazing what some people throw away, one trip we made turned out to be a lucky one although saying that, Tony nearly threatened to divorce me! This was our last trip of the day and we were both knackered, as I was chucking rubbish into the dump, something caught my eye, (hello,) it was a rolled up carpet, after a little investigation, surprise, surprise, it turned out to be yellow, and wait for it, brand new! Had spirit people intervened? You should have seen the look on Tony's face when I asked him sweetly to climb down into the dump, and lift the carpet out! (Old moaner!) If looks could kill I wouldn't be here now! Although we gave the carpet a good examination, we couldn't find a mark on it so the next job was to get it up the side of the dump, huffing and puffing, we weren't even sure if it would fit into our car, with the boot open, and the carpet pushed right up to the front window we got it in, (phew!) Several feet did still stick out the back and it meant that I had to sit in the boot, (great,) and hold the carpet in place to stop it falling out onto the road. Tony was still moaning on, and red in the face as he drove through the dump, going over every bump in the road (deliberately,) having to drive past the security guard on the gate didn't seem to help! Once we were home, and after checking my bruises, (ouch!) I won't say where! It was upstairs to see if it would fit our 12x10 group-room, a perfect fit! Had some-one bought to much and thrown this length away? Or had spirit materialized it, and arranged for us to be there at the right time? Whatever you may believe, it was the answer to our prayers!

Tony asked me never to tell a living soul where we had obtained the carpet, as he would act dumb, (that shouldn't be to hard then,) and deny all knowledge of it, the answer to that goes something like this, I speedily told all our friends, and as each members of our groups entered the group room, the first question I asked them was "do you like our carpet? We found it up the council dump, a present from spirit!"

It is so nice, and quite unbelievable the way that spirit can arrange these matters, how can we deny their little gifts to us?

That carpet witnessed many delightful evenings, and experienced so much spirit activity over the years, and was still wearing well when we moved. I wonder if it is still in place? It fitted into our group room lovely and I am sure that it helped to build up those unseen, but felt energies of spirit love, that were shared by all those that sat for development and meditation.

The one electric light bulb

The one electric light bulb in the group-room had blown; it sat in a purple coloured lamp shade on top of the music centre, and rather then go down stairs to get another one we decided to light a candle, have you ever watched a candle flame as it dances around, reflecting and casting shadows in the room, magic! As it illuminated the group room this particular evening the flame was growing taller and thinner like a piece of cotton almost reaching the ceiling, not all the way mind you as we did have polystyrene tiles fitted, what a fire hazard those dangerous things were, the cause of untold harm to people over the years! I say "Thank God for Artex!"

Getting back to that evening, we sat there, myself and four others listening to pan-pipe music and watching the candle flame as it danced about. We all felt very relaxed and as one as we do at these special meetings, when suddenly it was as if some-one had switched the light on! blazing fully almost blinding us, and bringing us out of our tranquil state with a jolt! Then as quickly as it had occurred we were back in semi darkness again, with just the candle glowing, we sat there for a few moments completely dumb-struck, lost for words!

What an evening! That bluey white blinding light could have only been spirit at work (play?), because as I mentioned earlier the only bulb in the group-room had blown! We sat chatting well past mid-night, and were all looking forward to next weeks group night with anticipation, maybe another happy memorable spirit experience was to come?

Another spiritual evening comes to mind, it was an extremely hot summers evening so we decided to leave the group-room door open, then settling down into our meditation mode so to speak, and switching off the calming music, a pin could be heard if dropped, the candle was sending lovely serene shapes around the room, suddenly there came from the landing outside the group-room this glorious bright light shooting across the ceiling towards us! It looked like mists folding upon folds above us radiating the most beautiful rainbow colours, then as quickly as it had appeared it was gone! Evaporated, disappeared! Not one of us had tried to reach up and touch it, we didn't even blink, it was as if we were stuck in some kind of time warp, meditation after that was impossible. I think it was Charlie, who was the first to speak and break our mesmerised state! Then all at once everyone was talking over each other, natter, natter. The static that was in the air was unbelievable, even Max our Doberman was plodding around the room in an excited state, woof, woof, no, he had already been out for his wee, wee, good boy! I forgot to mention that he always joined us in the group-room on these special nights, giving us many tell-tell signs that spirit were present, although he didn't actually have a tail, tail, ha, ha!

That lovely feeling of peace that we all felt followed us down stairs as we enjoyed cups of tea and biscuits and also puff, puff, cigarettes!

The next event I am about to tell you, is sure to make you laugh so please read on if you don't mind a couple of cracked ribs that is!

Burglars, we thought
Running a Spiritualist church (centre) can have its ups and downs; one of the biggest can be when the booked medium/speaker cancels at the last minute or as in this case the afternoon the only thing was for me to take the service myself, slight problem Tony was on a 2-10 shift ah! So it was on the phone to our very good friend, and vice president Charlie Atkins to arrange a lift and what a lovely evening it was too, many marvellous spiritual links made, and many happy faces.

On arriving back home I was just about to put the key in the door, which by the way was a glass panelled door when suddenly we saw a light shinning through the glass? Which can only be described as a torch light, it seemed to us that as soon as the light saw us it quickly went into the lounge area, we always left the door open for Max! Burglars we thought at the same time backing away from the door, there was no way we were going into the house, it was about 10.05pm so we sat on the wall outside to wait for Tony who came home from work at about 10.15pm.

When he pulled up and got out of the car he looked at us quizzically? We explained what we had seen. Tony followed by Charlie and I went up to the door and turned the key (gulp), which we had by the way left in the door in our hasty retreat, very dubiously we all walked in, when all of a sudden we were aware of some-thing, or some-one coming at us full speed, no time to turn and run, before Max our Doberman was all over us, waggling his little stumpy tail, woofey! Woofing, and grinning from ear to ear, in our panic we had completely forgotten about him being in the house (plonkers!) Burglars I don't think so? His bark could wake up the whole street, and as for his bite well we won't go there! We stood there and laughed, and laughed until our ribs hurt and then just to be on the safe side we searched the whole of the house, to check for any signs of a break-in, nothing! So what was that light?

Having just spoken to Charlie on the phone today 11 December 2006 he says he recalls that night like it was yesterday the biggest spirit orb we both agreed at least 3 inches round, how privileged we were to see it! Mind you a lot of people say that spirit orbs are specks of dust, ok!

We have been shown over the years many spirit orbs, spirit rods, and many spirit forms, some covered in ectoplasm! And luckily many of the spirit mists, and orbs we have managed to capture on video tape using an infa-red camera we still have those tape to this day! Would you like to see them?

Our evenings of physical phenomena, have given to many absolute proof of life after death...spirit life! There have been many trance talks and lots of touchings, feeling the webby substance of ectoplasm, that might to you sound creepy but it is a gift from spirit, and I say to you it is done in "God's all powerful name"

Hopefully you all enjoyed reading, "burglars we thought" Read on about our very good friend Charlie Atkins own life... (Charlie is my brother from another life long since gone!) you may find interesting the next few paragraphs written in his own words.

My story by Charles Atkins

Back in November 2006 Ann had told me that she fully intended to finish writing her book, I believe she started it back in the eighties, it was to contain her memoirs, and spiritual experiences, and she asked me if I would like to write a few lines, so here goes. I feel that there is only one place to start and that is way back to my teenage years, crank, crunch, that's the memory in gear! What's that saying about being as old as you feel?

When I was in secondary school my best mate came from Teynham a beautiful part of Kent, that was to be my introduction to that area, and after many visits I had the feeling that one day I would live there, I had this feeling with me for years and years, on my visits it always felt as though I was coming home, there were many times as I walked around Teynham that I thought, "I'm sure I have been across this road or that bridge before?"

As my teenage years passed by (sob) and life progressed as it does I eventually met the love of my life, and got married, we moved to South

Tankerton, my wife and I settled very happily into our new home, well it wasn't a new house just a new home to us. It was exciting starting out onto our new pathway together, decorating and going out to buy little bits of furniture putting our stamp on the place you could say, what more could we ask for? Some years later one of my work-mates was looking through the local paper, and came to the property section, he was reading out loud details of an empty property which had a back garden measuring 175ft long, I had missed my garden since we had moved, having lived in the country for the largest part of my life so far, another exciting detail was that the house was situated in Teynham my favourite part of Kent.

I took the paper home with me to show my wife, who was very interested as it meant me being closer to my place of work, less time spent travelling, I wouldn't have to get up so early especially in the winter months which in turn meant more time spent together a decision was made and we went to view the house, which we both instantly fell in love with, we put our offer in there and then! There was one big problem though 3 other people had already put offers in, one of those being a work-mate…ouch, and one being a cash buyer.

We went ahead and put our house on the market in the mean time thinking it would take awhile to sale, we had a buyer and a sold sign up within two weeks! Crikey! We decided that we had better view some other properties, and were getting a little worried when we could not find one we both liked, but as it turned out we shouldn't have worried, we got the house in Teynham, and moved in a few weeks later.

Unbeknown to us the next door neighbour was a man named Bill Ryan who just happened to be the president of the local Spiritualist church, don't we often ask ourselves if there is such a thing as coincidence? To that question I have to answer no! no! Certainly not!

After awhile we became very friendly and during our many conversations the subject of Spiritualism came up, surprise, surprise, and although he never pressured me in any way shape or form, my interest in the subject was growing the meetings were held every Monday 6.30-8pm in due course he invited me to come along. So this particular Monday evening off I went with no expectations but feeling a little apprehensive.

On arriving and opening the door at the stated time, what a shock I got. I had apparently gone along on the wrong Monday, oops! What a dopey date I am, in the hall were ladies of various ages and sizes, and yes wearing leotards they were the majorettes, or some other dancing troupe practising their routines! I stood there thinking "This is a strange Spiritualist church" I made my apologies, and was out of there like a shot.

This didn't deter me, and the following week, on the correct Monday I went along and happily joined in with all the others at the meeting.

From the platform the medium was introduced, and after saying an opening prayer we sang a hymn that was followed by a little talk on Spiritualism, another hymn, me with my croaky voice! Then followed the clairvoyance where messages were given out, there was many communicating links made, and many happy faces that night! Although I must add that I didn't receive a message, my feelings were quite mixed about the whole evening and on reflection I can say I was not overly impressed. I still had an open mind and went along the next week, and what outstanding messages I received, the medium mentioned a Triumph motorbike and a gentleman that had three successive heart attacks the last one fatal, taking him to the spirit world. That message among others was absolutely correct. I could barely open my mouth to utter y-y-yes, there was no-one there who knew me, there's no way anyone could have known these things especially the medium who had travelled from outside the area. I was truly amazed, intrigued, is this what Spiritualism was about proving that there was life after death?

Charlie and the revamped bike

By the way I still have that Triumph motor bike and have recently had it revamped this was the beginning for me, after that night I became a devout Spiritualist not missing a meeting unless I was working an awkward shift, every meeting attended and many messages received. Ta! I was so happy I must have looked like a grinning hyena; all my doubts and apprehensions gradually dwindled away.

It seemed that spirit people were keeping me very interested indeed no not in any forceful way but in away that only our inner being understands love light and care!

Around this time I started to question the whereabouts of other Spiritualist churches, and found out that there was another quite close by in a neighbouring town where several of the congregation from Teynham would some times go, I became friendly with several of the members there, and this helped me to open up from my shyness, especially as we always had nice little chats afterwards. One evening a lady asked the male medium who had just taken the service "how do you go about joining a development circle?" the gentleman in question replied "you are sitting in a circle now!!" we then noticed that we had unconsciously moved our seats into a circle, adding here that there was a lady who ran development groups for both churches. The circle sat regularly every week although only a handful of people, it was held most importantly in harmony during this period and with my own development. I was well happy.

Watch this space
One Monday the president of the church gave out in the notices that a psychic supper was to be held on the Isle of Sheppey! To be honest I didn't really feel as though I needed a reading, but the event was going to be in aid of charity, so I decided to place my name on the notice board along with all the others that were interested.

The psychic supper evening soon came around; we were all very excited as we arrived at the conservative hall,as there was a bar I got myself a drink (non-alcoholic!) yes really! As later I was off to work; I was standing there, no not propping it up, and I was asking "which medium was going to be on our table" friends pointed to a lady over the other side of the room, "that's her" they said "her name is Ann Turner" as I looked over guess what my first impression was? I thought that she looked like a witch and think that I actually voiced this out loud,sorry Ann! There was seven of us to each table, and the medium came round to each of us in turn, to give us an individual reading, the first thing she mentioned to me was a family of five (my family) that was the first of many wonderful spiritual messages that she gave that evening after she had completed all the readings around the table we all got stuck into some yummy! Food, munch, munch! Ann said that if we wanted to we could ask questions, and she would do her best to answer! ...I had a few that I had been searching the answers to, mind you it wasn't for the lack of asking, it was just the fact that a lot of the answers I had been given so far didn't seem to completely satisfy me. To my amazement Ann managed to answer all my questions that night so much so that as I left the hall to go to work, I punched the air in elation. I felt on top of the world!

This feeling stayed with me all through the night-shift, and for many weeks to follow, happy, happy, Charlie boy!

That was the first time I had met or heard of Ann Turner, she made such an impact on me that I just had to have her telephone number, so I phoned the president of the town church, who was very reluctant to give me her number, as she respected Ann's privacy, but cheeky chappy Charlie was very persistent, and explained that it was a matter of life or death and she eventually gave into me! Hooray!

Plucking up the courage I telephone her and would you believe it she repeated all the things about her privacy that the president of Sheppey church had said to me, oops!

Many years later and serving as a Spiritualist medium myself I understood the importance of her words about privacy, and understood that we all have lives to live outside of Spiritualism!

It was suggested, in the short conversation that I write down any questions I had, and if I wanted to I could come over to their home once a month, and Ann would try to answer my spiritual enquires! After replacing the receiver the emotions that I felt at that time were overwhelming, its hard for me to describe in words just how I felt!

A while later Ann was invited to the church circle to help develop/ teach us up and coming young protegees. One particular evening during meditation spirit wanted to take me off somewhere to show me something as they often did, but I refused to go, digging my heels firmly in! Being a right so and so that I can be!

The following week, when the group met for meditation, I decided that I was going to go off into meditation on my own – big mistake! Although I didn't realise it at the time, we were always given a symbol to meditate on as a group, collectively one of the golden rules of development. I had other ideas so off I went on my own following this bluey white light, no problems so far! Moving faster and faster, just as I thought that I had caught it up, it increased in speed again no way could I even get close by now I began to feel as though I was swimming, flapping my arms in a way a bird does when flying travelling millions, trillions of miles, and I was on my own let me remind you, my choice! The next thing I recall was hyper-ventilating having been thrown onto the floor, wham, bang, feeling as near to death as was possible, believe me.

Somehow Ann had come into my meditation consciousness and bought me back having somehow known of my dilemma, she knew that I had gone off totally alone, a very dangerous thing to do when you first start sitting for meditation/development, my guide was only to pleased to go along with my wishes ...what a painful invaluable lesson I had learnt something never to be repeated or forgotten! I feel certain that had Ann not bought me back out of that meditation I would have certainly joined my loved ones in the spirit world!

The next day I could hardly move my arms, how many miles had I travelled in that experience? Spirit vibration as we know is timeless!

I say this to you my friends, always do as you are asked when in development circle, until the time comes that you and your guide are more in tune, understanding and in harmony with each other never try to run before you can crawl! Right up to this day, 16 December 2006, I have no idea how Ann managed to bring me out of that meditation? All I know is "Thank God" she did.

During this period of my development I became a very emotional person, which lasted for about eighteen months, many times I was out of control, especially within the circle, night times were a living hell for me a most tortuous period in my life!

In my mind I was leaving my wife, my children and the house and going to live on my own in my old motor home! I was prepared to give up every thing, I was living this all in my mind, my family never realised what I was going through, or what I was thinking

On one occasion during this very emotional time I was convinced that I had somehow upset Ann, by simply saying one word out of turn. I just had to pick up the phone and call her, I was a wreck, lower then the lowest, not even fit to crawl in the gutter. I blurted out all my feelings and thoughts I felt as though I had no-one in the whole wide world to turn to. Ann listened, and spoke to me many comforting words of reassurance she explained that she had been through similar feelings herself many times during her life of never ending development, she assured me that I certainly had not in any way shape or form offended her.

I felt so much better after speaking to her (at length) a lot more like my old self, so I say to you my friends don't keep those stressful feelings to your self, bend a family/ friends ear you will feel so much better for sharing it... You will feel 100% better I promise you after the release of those pent up emotional energies!

A little while later Ann was invited to take a couple of venues at a spiritual workshop on the Rock of Gibraltar at Ray Smith's spiritual centre. She told me about it and asked if I would like to go? What do you think I replied, yes, yes, yes please! Then arranging with a work mate to change his holiday rota, which by the way, was not an easy thing.

It was arranged that we all meet up at Standsted airport, eight of us altogether on what we called the Gibraltar-trip!

One night in my sleep state spirit showed me exactly where Ann and I would be sitting on the aeroplane, at the time I wasn't even sure whether I would be able to go myself, but obviously spirit knew in advance.

I stayed at Tony and Ann's home the night before, as Tony was driving us to the airport the next day, here are some extracts taken from my diary written while at the spiritual centre, flying was a great experience for me, my first flight in a jet propelled aircraft.

During the flight Ann and I went over some of my old writings, half of which had long been forgotten about, but it was something I felt was well worth doing. I felt this was going to be a great week, with much knowledge, wisdom and learning shared.

We arrived at the centre and were shown our sleeping quarters; I felt a bit cut off from the main party as I was situated on the ground floor all on my own, although I did have my own private bathroom just across the passage from my room.

Our host advised us on the coming weeks events that were planned for us, talks, videos, and shows covering, I ching, Numerology and Tarot, among others. The video that was shown to us was about faces appearing, and changing on rocks, at remote village in Spain, the House of Rocks is called "Cuesta Carres" which means Hill of Faces!

Also shown on the video was out of body experiences which all seemed to make sense to me!

In the evening there was a demonstration of flower sentience, earlier in the day we had been asked to find a flower, and bring it along with us to see if it could be read, my curious mind was wondering? I choose a thistle type flower with a deeply enclosed centre, which I wrapped up delicately the number of my flower was 52 and guess what? Mine among others was chosen after my flower was picked out, the medium turned sideways on to us not even looking up, not even knowing whom she was with, or reading.

This is what I received delicately wrapped, feels that this person needs to be cushioned, has had a very hard life, who is sensitive but also very deep, can be easily hurt, serious and loyal, needs to be held, and cuddled, a fragile person who keeps the true self within, the jolly and outgoing attitude is to protect this person from others, feel this person needs healing although more of the soul, then the physical being, this person is very creative with their hands (my vegetable plot and flower garden,) this person loves going to the theatre, but not as much as they used to, they also love music, love to walk in the woods, surrounding themselves with trees, told also of a nervous problem with the back, but have not been able to place that to this day? This person also carries a lot of grief now, and from the past (passing of my sister Dorothy). I feel this person needs more love about them, I most certainly do, all perfectly true, wow!

I never said that the person receiving the messages was me until after the readings were over, then I sheepishly owned up, at the same time wishing that the floor would open up and swallow me, my emotions were very close to the surface, all this time I was feeling emotional, I just wanted to get up and leave, what she had given to me was absolutely amazing, never before had I been got so deeply! After sharing this special part of my life with you, from so long ago I would like to say one final word getting to me, as really gotten to me.

There was a evening of table phenomena, where a group of four people placed their hands on top of a table. There was no response from the first four people, so their places were then taken by four new people, it was then my turn, after placing my hands on the table I was aware of such warmth and power, a lady called Janet then asked if there was "Anyone there" who wished to talk with us? Nothing no reply! "Is there anyone there who wishes to speak to Charles?" My mind became filled with light the table started to tilt towards me, I just knew that it was my sister feeling very emotional, the alphabet was being counted A.B.C., etc by this time there was a lot of conversation taking place between my sister and I both verbally and mentally which I can't disclose here, it is too private, as you will understand! Something's I will mention are, the fact that it was said they are helping with all situations around me including my wife, I was told that we would be together until the end and the end never comes! I thanked my sister asking her to except all my love as always and to say "Hello" to all our relatives, adding to this I feel we could have got up during all this, and at any time moved the table wherever we wished by just holding our palms face down on it. I told my sister that we all loved and missed her physical presence and to go now but most of all be free! Enjoy your life in the spirit-world! I look forward to your future visits the emotion just flowed out of me, if you knew my sister and I you would understand why!

There were many more spiritual experiences during that Workshop holiday that drew on my emotions and sensitivities.

Another night during my stay my whole bedroom filled with an unconditional love a thousand times more powerful in its intensity then earthy love, an untold number of tears flowed from my eyes that night words just can not express the feeling!

At breakfast the next morning I felt and looked like a complete wreck which seemed to be the story of my life, back then, thankfully now I have complete control!

Ann suggested to me that I go back to bed, so without making to much fuss off I went, during this rest period I experienced Ann's very powerful healing guide drawing close…which helped me to drop off into a lovely refreshing sleep, when I awoke I felt so much better, in fact I felt like a new man.

There was plenty of time for us all to relax during the day, so Ann and I set off for a long stroll along the beach, which if I recall correctly was almost deserted, we made friends with a dog that didn't seem to want to leave us, as we strolled along we recounted the many experiences that we had shared on this trip so far, experiences that will never ever be forgotten even the bartering at the local market brings back happy memories, my bartering skills were non-existent, so I had to rely on

Ann to secure us both presents for our families, no not rubbish stuff! Although she was excellent at bartering, her sense of direction was terrible if we depended on her to get us home we would probably ended up lost never to be seen again!

The whole trip from beginning to end was an absolute joy, a very special week that will stay in my mind for ever.

On our arrival back to the UK, Tony was there to meet us at the airport, I feel we must have given him an ear-ache as we both did not stop nattering all the way home.

As I progressed with my development, I learned how to keep my emotions under control (lock and key) and I was invited to join one of Ann's advanced circles. My confidence was starting to grow now although only still at a snails pace, I decided that I wanted to become more involved and started to go to Tony and Ann's spiritual centre, helping to lay up the hall in preparation for the service, making cups of tea and sometimes chairing for the serving medium. I was also promoted to Vice president none of this however would have taken place if it were not for my dearest friend Ann, she was a brick in every sense of the word, during the many hard lessons that I had to learn. Ann was very disciplined in her teachings allowing no nonsense she was always truthful, honest and above all genuine!

The teachings were changing becoming more of a higher level, we, my guide and I started to work more as a team as one. Information was being shared from the Teacher of the group, Ann's guide and good friend "Chang" preparing me for that little step up on to the platform (rostrum) to share an evening of clairvoyance and psychic art with Ann and Tony, questions, questions, could I do this? Would my nerves let me down? Was I being thrown in at the deep end? Would I sink or swim?

Before the service we stopped off at a friends of Tony and Ann's whom they had arranged to visit, and had something to eat, the apartment was situated upstairs, my nerves were shot to pieces (gulp) so much so that I could not eat a thing, and I swear to God that if the veranda windows had been opened I think I would have probably jumped!

Even though I was so stressed and nervous the evening went quite well, in Ann's words brilliant! This was simply the beginning of many more services to come. Word of mouth spread, and recommendations, introductions were made gradually, slowly over the years building up my own services with many different Spiritualist churches and centres!

Ann and I have become more and more like brother and sister and have much trust and respect for each other. Over the years sitting in circle in complete harmony we have shared many magical happenings, and I have learnt so much, life is extremely good!

One very snowy evening
One very snowy evening taking Ann to a service at Crawley in my motor-home, the church rang to ask if we were still coming? Yes! Ann replied.

What an horrendous journey we had that night, we must either of been mad or so dedicated that we didn't want to let spirit down, or disappoint the church, during our journey the water bottle froze, and the heater packed up making seeing out very difficult in the heavy snow fall, when we pull up outside the church there was at least eight inches of snow on the road, so we had to park where we could. When we entered the church...Would you believe it! There was at least fifty people gathered bless them, they had all like us made an effort to be there. We were welcomed with thunderous applause and a well needed cup of hot tea and what a truly spiritual evening we all shared!

The journey home was just as hazardous the weather turned worse, snow blizzards, and they were starting to close the roads, thank God that the service had been cut short so everyone could travel home. Our journey home was the biggest night-mare, slipping and sliding struggling to see where we were going, then the window wipers packed up, and as the water bottle was frozen we had to stop every few hundred yards to clear the snow from the wind screen, yes definitely a night-mare, after dropping Ann off and eventually arriving home myself, my eyes were aching with the strain of keeping the motor-home on the road, never in my entire life have I been so please to see the sight of my own front door, and to be safely home I said the biggest thank you to spirit as I know without them we would never have made it. Ann was very relieved to hear my voice when I phone to let her know that I was home in one piece safe and sound.

Thinking back now I really don't know how we stayed on the road that night!

I know one thing, the weather-man should get his facts right he never forecast/predicted such atrocious weather, but I thank spirit once again for looking after us!

Weeks, months, year after year Ann, Tony and I sat devotedly in our circle with spirit friends, for the development of physical phenomena we called ourselves the three musketeers, and still do to this day.

Because of Ann's failing health we had to call a halt to the circle, I however still visited and we had some lovely spiritual conversations, over many cups of tea, and with what we like to call, snackler plates of goodies yum, yum.

I had the feeling that Ann and Tony were going to move, to Wales and they were, as you can imagine this meant breaking up the three musketeers, I wished them well, it was not for me to try and influence them to stay although I wanted to,believe me! We all have many different pathways to walk!

The day of the move was a night-mare in its self, but that's another story. I drove their Nissan car while they drove their VWcamper-van, we travelled over-night, the next day when it came time for me to travel back home to Kent I found most difficult, I can't write down words to express my feelings at that time.

We have since then met up on several occasions, especially when they have been invited to take services back in Kent, or at Xmas when they sometimes visit their families and friends, our meetings were brief barely enough time to say "Hello".

But on the 16th October 2006 I visited them in Wales, and what a group reunion that was, the whole stay was wonderful, never a dull moment spiritually, or materially, on one of our many outings we went to Llansteffan Castle, and what a beautiful walk it was through the woody area to the castle, many photos were taken of each other, the scenery, and castle what a lovely enjoyable day that was, when we arrived back home and down-loaded the photos on to the PC, there were so many taken, but one in particular caught our eye, we were so utterly amazed to see a photo taken whilst we were walking huffing and puffing up the steep walk way leading to the castle, unaware that Tony hanging back, camera in hand, had snapped this particular photo which showed a twin orb in flight beside of us which we found absolutely incredible, once again proof that spirit are always present, could Tony be a psychic photographer? Time however passed by to quickly as it always does when your having fun, although our lives have moved on in so many different ways with so many incredible opportunities.

Charlie and me plus the twin orb on the left at Llansteffan Castle

    I treasure our time together, and know I would never change my life given the chance. I feel that if I hadn't met Ann my spiritual life would not have been possible! Mind you what is two hundred mile away when you have BT anytime third option?

    We give each other an ear-ache (ouch!) with our three hour phone calls, and mumbles and grumbles, we also keep in touch using our mobiles texting. So much so I would say that we bridged that gap as perfect brother and sister, no-one and nothing can ever change that! And I thank spirit and Ann from my very soul for this life.

    I have only tipped into a tiny part of my life, but know this, all life is precious be happy and live it to the full make the most of each and every moment, God Bless.

Guiding Orb

Of all the stupid places to have a light switch, ours was situated not by the front door as you came in, but right at the other end of the very long passage way, which meant walking into the house and fumbling in the dark for the switch!

This particular night/early hours of the morning Tony and I had just arrived home after some horrendous motorway driving, we were knackered and the only thing that was on our minds was bed and blissful sleep!

On entering the house and stumbling (ouch!) along the passageway, trying to find the light switch, we witnessed the most incredible sight, slowly coming down the stairs towards us, it was the brightest, teeny weeny orb like light so beautifully sparkling like a star, lighting up the dark passageway, we stood there both dumbstruck with amazement, watching it as it came forward and began to circle around us, wow! The darkness had completely disappeared as this little beautiful orb slowly but with intelligence moved towards the light switch, we were mesmerised, we hadn't spoken a word to each other, both just staring transfixed on this little orb! As it carefully made its way back up the stairs heading towards our special spiritual room, as it slowly disappeared out of our sight, we were standing there in the passage way like a pair of statues in a blaze of electric light, all thoughts of sleep were suddenly gone! We stayed up until it was almost light waffling, and drinking tea, what an absolutely beautiful experience we had shared! When we went up those very stairs (eventually) to bed following in the orbs path, we popped into our special grouproom for a moment, and although we could not now see it we could certainly feel the lovely spirit energies that surrounded us, magic!

Over the years we have had the privilege to witness many beautiful, sparkling orbs of all shapes and sizes, many of which we have been able to catch/record on camera and video tape!! But sadly our little guiding orb of that night as never appeared to greet us again, and yes! Wonders will never, cease, Tony after years of me asking (nagging!) eventually moved that stupidly placed light switch nearer to the front door, yippee!

CHAPTER 10

The gift of healing

Animals not only give us immense joy, happiness, loyalty, and loving companionship, but also laughter which doesn't seem to be about so much these days!

In my opinion, although you may disagree? They posses such healing power and are very psychic, even more so then most of us human beings!

Pets such as cats and dogs are now allowed to visit their owners in some hospitals, and other caring establishments, some nursing homes which look after those of more advanced years also welcome the visit of pets to help keep their guests uplifted and happy. It is now well known that stroking a cat or dog or any of our furry friends and exchanging those feelings of love and affection can bring about peace and calm and can also lower ones blood pressure to a healthy level.

Us humans have been charged with the responsibility of looking after all God's creatures. In addition to receiving all that they give us we are also endowed with our own gifts which enable us to help them in their needs, my own healing powers have been called upon many times to help sick or poorly animals and of course human beings as well!

Healing is the greatest of all God's gifts, it is such an immense privilege to be used as a divine channel.

It is pure undiluted love, understanding of another's pain whether human or animal, such as when a child falls down and hurts its knee and we rub it better, isn't that natural healing love?

We are all like bombs of energy. Could we gather together, and help heal the world, of all its miseries, pain, and hunger, also cleanse our rivers and greenery, or even mend the hole in our sky (ozone layer)?

Healing love being the most explosive and precious gift that all of us, God's children have been blessed with.

Western thinking in these matters has now progressed to the point where the British Medical Association in its wisdom now recognises and accepts spiritual healing by touch! It also allows registered healers to visit patients in hospitals when requested, it there for accepts that spiritual healers have a complimentary role to play along side doctors and nurses.

Isn't it nice that man can heal, and help many in pain, and work side by side in harmony throughout the world!

If only everyone knew of the benefits to be gained, even those people who are aware of spiritual healing are however often reluctant to ask for help for themselves, or their animal friends until it is almost becomes a matter of life and death, what is that saying? nothing ventured, nothing gained exactly.

Neighbours Alison and Simon
Our good friends, popped in one day they were very upset, it seemed that their pussy cat named Treacle had apparently been involved in an accident to her back legs and she couldn't walk, she was taken to the vets, but they could not be sure what the problem was, and said that perhaps her kidneys were failing, or that she had damage to her spine! Although they had been living next door for some years, and on occasion had questioned, and listened to some of our spiritual adventures, they like a lot of others were still quite sceptical understandably so, and a little afraid of the unknown as we all are at times.

Even so when desperate and unsure and with no-one to turn to they held their scepticism in check, and for the sake of their pussy cat, meow, purr, purr, asked for help, so over a nice cup of tea they explained all about Treacle and her visit to the vets, once they had relaxed and were less upset they went home, with us promising to pop in later that evening.

Visiting them later that evening, yes more cups of tea, gurgle, and more chat, at the same time giving Treacle lots of cuddley strokes and loving kisses which she seemed to enjoy immensely, purr, purr, meowww.

We left Alison and Simon that evening with cheery hearts, and the promise that we would pop in again the next day.

This happened on the 26th October 1990, and the vet said that if there was no improvement in her condition in a couple of days, to bring her back.

The next day as promised I popped in to see pussy cat Treacle, and give more loving cuddles and caresses, I could feel her relaxing to the touch, meow! Purr! their other cat Bagpuss was there also sitting, looking up at me as if to say "what you again Aunty Ann, can I have some cuddles too" I forgot to mention, Alison and Simon were at work when I popped in, this wasn't a problem as we had each others door keys, so that when we went away on holiday we could each look after one another's houses and baby-sit each others cats. Going in day after day she started to show slow, but sure signs of improvement, much to Alison and Simon's happiness, when they did take her back to the vets for an examination it revealed that she had made a complete recovery. They were so pleased that they decided that they could after all go away for a previously booked weekend without worry and stress!

No matter, whatever you think of this little story, please at the same time, and with an open mind always know that love can conquer much, and that spirit people are always there to help and assist us.

As for the healing power, when it passes through my hands it is almost like electrical energy, my hands seem to know which part of the body needs that healing love, and they are drawn to that area, other times my eyes are like x/rays and its as if I can see into the patience body and see where I need to place my hands, or use my mind to operate and remove the causes of pain without the use of instruments, we are all channels for healing love!

It has often been said that my hands, during healing feel extremely hot, like two little irons, I remove them if I feel the person or animal is uncomfortable, like with Treacle when she pulled herself away (no longer dragging her back legs) I knew she could feel the heat.

Cats like other animals have their own personality for instance Treacle likes to be petted and stroked, but Bagpuss is more independent and chooses those times when she wants attention, Alison and Simon have both felt the heat that comes off of my hands, and were truly elated by Treacle's. recovery

Do you have certain gifts? I can only speak of my own experiences of spirit, and they have certainly showed me without a doubt that there is an unseen energy at work and that life goes on, there is no death, simply an extension to life everlasting, that's my opinion!

I can't say for sure when in my life these different gifts developed themselves. It comes to me that like my spirit friends, they have always been there to help and give others assistance, I feel that we are all placed here to help each other, and that there are no coincidences, everything and everyone that we meet are there for a reason, as if our lives have been mapped out, perhaps they have?

When Alison and Simon first acquired their pussy cats Treacle and Bagpuss from the cat's home, they took them to the vets for their jabs against flu and other nasties etc:

After a couple of days poor Treacle went off her food and Alison noticed that her jaw was stuck, and although she was trying to eat, her jaw just didn't move, Alison feared the worst, it seemed to us all that she had suffered an heart attack, on taking her to the vets this was confirmed for apparently poor Treacle had an underlying heart condition that was triggered off by the flu jab.

Every day I went in to help nurse Treacle back to health, if possible that is, after two weeks or so she got over her problems and started to eat, almost eating them out of house and home, which can be seen by the size of her big fat belly, meow!

Alison hesitates and worries every year when the vet's appointment comes around but Treacle has never had a recurrence of her heart condition. I always thank God after giving healing and for using me, my heart, mind and hands, and for allowing those divine energies to flow.

Our very life is in Gods hands and in both these cases if it was time for Treacle to join her cat family, and friends in the spirit world she would have. But whatever the outcome it would have been nice for her to receive all the love, kisses, and cuddles, she's such a big sloppy cat.

Although not always, I do sometimes feel a little tired after giving healing. It is my life's privilege to serve the spirit people for as long as possible.

I derive great pleasure and happiness from knowing that animals in all their innocence have benefited and become well and healthy once again after receiving healing. When humans are similarly healed my joy is also overwhelming and I am sometimes held in awe and wonderment over what has been achieved, but it simply proves that nothing is impossible with the limitless and bounteous love shared, miracles can and do happen!

Also remember that prayers and thoughts are living energies which go out from us into the unseen world to be acted upon. We have the remarkable ability in our minds to be able to change much in our physical world and so we must master our thoughts and use them wisely and only for good.

Ann's villa in Spain

My Mum and Lisa in Malaga

Harry Australia

I would like to share one particular miracle with you, well that's what all concerned called it, you may think differently?

It occurred when Tony and I went to Spain for a fortnight's holiday some years ago, and we were staying at our friend Ann's house in Malaga, a beautiful old castle style home, adding here that we were baby sitting her boxer dog Lisa, while Ann visited her home town of Manchester in England.

We were both truly ready for this break and to have a rest away from the stress, and strain, pleasing ourselves as people do on holiday.

There was no strict regimes, no time schedules, eat and drink when ever we wanted, lay around and sleep late, yawn, yawn, sunbathe and generally enjoy ourselves, maybe a little bit of sight seeing, and yes! downing, a few Spanish beers (hic!).

We were very fortunate that the beach was only across the road from where we were staying, so with no lengthy journey or travelling to do we just strolled across the road to the beach every day to enjoy a swim and laze around in the Spanish sunshine. We ate our lunch at the beach bar which was sheltered from the midday sun, bliss!

No matter where we have journeyed or whatever the circumstances Tony could always switch off his working motor, relax completely and forget everything easy peasy for him, like turning off a tap.

I have often commented on this and thought how lucky he is, as for myself, I find it practically impossible to completely 100% switch off After a couple of days into the holiday we met some very nice people who we continued to meet every day.

Its funny, but it seems to me that no matter where we go, or whatever part of the world we may visit, there are always people who it would seem are just waiting to meet spiritually minded people, and this holiday was no exception, do you know what I mean?

Australian Harry in Spain

This is the holiday that we met Harry!
It happened quite naturally, and I say this as we are great believers that there is no such thing as "chance" were we meant to meet Harry? We certainly believe so.

Harry was an Australian man who was staying in an apartment for six months; he had flown over from Aussie land to help him recover from a serious operation he had under gone a few months before.

He was very modest about it indeed, obviously he was still feeling the emotional stress that he had suffered months earlier, after much encouragement he went on to explain that he had suffered two brain tumours and this was the second operation that he been through in the last three years. He explained that the original tumour was a female, and could not be completely removed ever, and had grown again after the first operation, his braveness was overwhelming, words fail me!

His doctors had advised him against flying to Malaga, as they felt that he would probably not make it.

You see his skull was very thin, and after two operations there wasn't a lot of bone left, they said that if he insisted on going then he should be told the consequences, his skull could in actual fact collapse! The words Harry used were "cave in".

He was such a joker always happy and smiling and with a true sense of humour, why at times we laughed so much we felt our ribs would break he was always in high spirits and had a whale of a time. Yes, he liked a jug or two of sangria, or whatever else was on offer!

This courageous man, the life and soul of the party, a very special person he joined in all the activities, even though he was on crutches at the time, the bar held a lot of events, and he was not going to miss out on any of the fun, no way was he.

He was probably one of the bravest men we have ever had the privilege to know!

During our many conversations it came out that I was a Spiritualist medium and registered healer. Although he didn't really understand all about these matters he was still a great believer in "unseen forces" and asked if I would give him healing on his toes, which he had been unable to move for about three years since the first operation.

He jokingly said that his toes had suffused together like webs, not a pretty sight; they looked like a pair of flippers, we called him Harry the sea merchant mind you they did have there uses, they were his biggest asset for swimming, he could move through the water like a fish.

We used to laugh with him when he went down to the sea to have a swim, this rather tall (6 foot 6 or so) heavily built man on crutches wobbling down like a duck, a bit like what you see in comic strips we all laughed so much with him, what happy times!

It was agreed that, first thing in the morning, and the last thing at night I would administer healing love, placing my hands about one inch away from his head and feet (not massaging), that was the beginning.

On the third day when Harry came down to the beach his face looked like a childs. He was so excited, his face beaming like a Cheshire cat, you could see that he was not acting, it was like all his Christmases and birthdays had come at once. He sat down and showed us his toes, he could actually move them separately not all lumped together, but separately!

You can imagine his joy at being able to move his toes again after such a long time.

We all simply stared in amazement, had we all shared in a miracle?? What else could it be?

The look on Harry's face will stay with us for the rest of our lives, it was as if he had been given a new toy for Christmas, a new pair of feet Ha!Ha! He kept saying in his Aussie twang "it's a bloody miracle" and kept hugging us, it wasn't as if he was a little man, and with me being quite tiny he nearly squeezed the life out of me, seriously!

We remember back to that day with such delight, in fact the whole holiday gives us ultimate evidence, that "to give is to receive" and if by placing one's hands on a person or animal, with God Almighty's love gives so much happiness, and relief of pain, and stress then may I always have the healing power to help all those in the world (I think I had better get six pairs of hands, for mine are soon going to wear out,) what do you think?

Continuing with his daily morning, and evening healing sessions, Harry's toes by the end of the holiday began to move perfectly normal The other friends who shared this special holiday, included Sandra, Sue and her husband John, who lived in Brighton, there were others but unfortunately I can't recall their names. We also met Limbo, who gave healing massages whilst on the beach; he used to entertain us by doing acrobatics, I think he was probably double jointed, he was from Venezuela.

Everyday he would bring a natural yogurt to give me extra energy, he was a very spiritual man, they say it takes one to know one, and in Limbo's case this was quite true.

He said it always shows in the eyes, funny I always thought of myself as a bit cross-eyed looking!

At the end of the holiday, Jose and Juan the people who own Sugar Beach Bar, held a going away party for us all, there was lots to celebrate especially as we had all witnessed Harry's toes moving again, and we had all become very close friends, we all promised that we would meet up again at the same place, late in October if it was at all possible! There was the usual exchange of addresses and phone numbers etc; and then came the jugs of sangria, what a fantastic time we had shared, and what a lovely end to our holiday. Such happiness, but also some sadness thinking, we might never meet again.

We all spoke for hours about mediumship and Spiritualism, particularly Harry he was very interested, and had so many questions. Before parting on our last night it was suggested to Harry that he think of us at a certain time, and we would also think of him, surrounded in loving healing energy, this I did regularly for the next five months, yes we did all meet up again in October and surprise, surprise, Harry looked the picture of health, toes still moving, and with no crutches we hardly recognised him!

I thank God, for we knew that his healing power had most certainly been at work, and that all our prayers had been answered.

Although Harry believed that this was a little miracle, could it have been his own inner spirit? Self healing and determination that had brought about such a change? Something for you to think about!

How could we ever forget that year, and all friends that we had met, especially Harry? And the very emotional time that we all shared with him, the memory will stay with us forever, what a privilege to be part of God's world, and knowing that spirit life share their loving thoughts, always only a breath away!

That time spent with our friends went by so quickly (sigh) returning home we felt extremely good within ourselves, looked rested, suntanned, and revitalized.

Harry also returned home to Australia, as October was the end of his six months recuperation period, he promised us that he would phone after he had visited his consultant at the hospital.

It was such a worrying time, as we kept thinking about Harry, and his flight home, it was such along haul, were we being a little negative?

All the time Chang was whispering "do not worry" he will be ok, and arrive home safely!

They were the longest three weeks of our life's, then Harry phoned, magic! His consultant was truly amazed, that not only was Harry alive and kicking, but was also in such excellent health, and that his skull was still intact! He also witnessed the movement in his toes, and the fact that he was not using crutches, looking totally like a new man, to hear such fantastic news was brilliant, to say the least we were elated, and overjoyed, our emotions flowed just incredible. Thank you God!

"This is Ann Turner"

Even after Harry had returned to Australia, we would still think of him every night around 10.30, and send our loving healing thoughts to him, this went on for some time during which his condition, the brain tumour remained inactive, this was confirmed by the many phone calls we shared with him,yes! We did have some rather large phone bills as you can imagine.

Life goes on, we all travel our own pathway, we eventually lost contact with him, although over the years often spoke and thought of him, we wondered if Harry was still going strong, and living life to the full as only he could.

Whilst thinking about him I received two words "Phone Harry" much to my delight, mind you it could have been my imagination! No, that was my guardian angles voice, Chang, "thank you my dear friend". The thought was going through my mind, is Harry still with us, that was about 10.30 in the morning early November

Right, the next job I had on my hands, was to try and remember where I had put Harry's phone number and address? My mind was all over the place with so many excited thoughts, nothing unusual about that!

I knew the details were written down in an old diary, did I still have it?

The first place I looked was in an old bureau, which had three drawers, and you might say, much rubbish, upon opening the first drawer, there it was! beneath an old photo album, I have so many cupboards and drawers, and I keep promising myself to sort them out, but I never seem to have the time! Perhaps I will get around to it, one day!

Opening my old diary, I recalled many of the conversations that Harry and I shared my mind became a whirl (lovely) I also remember him telling us that although he had never married, he did have a lady friend whom he shared his life with back in Australia.

"So here goes", I picked up the phone dialled his number and waited, it was an answer machine, and a female voice was saying, "This is Ann Turner; please leave your name and number and I will get back to you". Ann Turner? They say that we all have a double! but the same name, I nearly dropped the receiver after hearing this women's voice, shocked I put the phone down, and lit up a cigarette I must say it did help, puff! Puff! It was quiet there wasn't as much as a whisper from my friends and family of the spirit life? Hellooooooo! However after sitting there for a while, and two cigarettes later, and smoking them through to the tip, naughty me! A thought came to me to ring Marcia our youngest daughter, whilst telling her about the phone call to Australia, and still feeling a bit shaken, she suggested ringing Harry in Australia for me, she was probably thinking "poor Mum has she at last flipped out" (gone off me rocker!) so in the circumstances it was probably best to humour me! Cheeky so and so!

If it were possible to smoke six cigarettes in a couple of minutes I would have done so, but I managed to contain myself and only smoke another two!

Marcia, having rang this so called Ann Turner called me back, although (it only took a few minutes, it seemed to me, like ages) to confirm she had also heard the same message! (Phew!) At least it proved to her that her Mum was still with it! For now anyway!

Next, we decided to check that we had both dialled the same number, and yes we had. Then came a fleeting thought, that maybe spirit were playing games, they often do you know? Marcia hung up after a while with a promise from me that I would let her know the outcome, that's if I could get to the bottom of it!

By now it was coming up to lunch time so I decided to get a snack, I am always hungry, little piggy me, oink!oink! no matter what the time of day or night it is! Yummy!

As I have mentioned before, our animals have always been able to sense our feelings, and by this time they were running up and down the lounge like crazy, woof, woof, meow, meow, or maybe they were just asking for their grub?

Spirit were very close, at this time, we all sensed them. So I thought I had better feed my hungry crazy furry friends, before they wore the carpets away, and then I made myself a sandwich, and a very sweet cup of tea, very sweet, they say that sweet tea is very good for shock or when there has been a drop in sugar levels, which as a Spiritualist medium seems to happen quite regularly.

Once I started to eat my sandwich, and drink my tea, I started to feel calm and relaxed, in came Chang's voice, "now that you are feeling better and more composed I will speak to you", was he in his way trying to tell me off? As he often does!

"Its alright for you" I hastily replied, forgetting that he himself had suffered many earthly conditions before going into the spirit world, he always called me "My little one" as though he were speaking to a child, but then I suppose I am with so many lessons to learn. One lesson was calmness, patience, and at times like this it was very hard indeed, but being my good companion, the better part of my life we understood each other and I didn't take offence, well I am not so sure about that!

It came into my mind to phone the overseas operator, (Thanks Chang!) anxious indeed I explained my plight to her, she offered to check the name, address, and number for me, same as before "Ann Turner" etc and yes I did have the right number and address, they were both registered to a Mr Wellman, which was Harry's surname.

This event sure did make the operators day unbelievable, we both laughed so much about it especially after I explained everything.

I imagine there was lots of chit-chat and laughs amongst the operators after I had hung up, probably thought I was some sort of crank?

It was suggested that I keep on ringing until either Harry or this so called "Ann Turner" returned home. As our phone had a two-way record button on it I decided to tape this woman's voice.

It was now 4.30pm, so I did some washing, and then prepared the dinner as Tony was due home from work shortly. I was so excited, I couldn't wait for him to hear the tape and tell him about the day's happenings!

What a laugh you must have been having Harry!

It was now about 8.30pm in England, Australia is about 10hrs ahead of us, "here goes" I thought as I picked up the phone to dial again, Tony sitting beside me for moral support (ear-wigging) but then I thought, ring tomorrow Chang's voice interrupts my thoughts, "call now my little one" I hesitated for a second, to late she had answered the phone, and I was speaking to "Ann Taylor" my two-way tape was on so our conversation was being recorded, this is how it went;

I asked the lady if I could speak to Harry Wellman please, she said that no-one of that name lived at this address??, thinking that this was a bit strange I quickly explained, that this was the phone number that Harry himself had given us, and that the international operator also had him registered at that number?

She then asked me to repeat his surname, Wellman! I replied. Then came down the line. "Oh Harry" in voice of sudden recognition and surprise, she went on to explain that Harry had passed away a few years earlier from a brain tumour whilst he was in England, further more she added how she used to visit Harry when he was in hospital, in Sydney, and that she was a good friend of his, which probably explained why he had given out her phone number, oh I see! I suppose that made sense? Still didn't explain how the address and phone were registered in his name though did it? Anyway the reason I had made contact, as you know was to enquire about Harry, and his well being, which of course I had, even though the news was sad to hear.

I thanked her for the information, and before hanging up we did have a little chuckle over her name "Ann Taylor" which when said with her slight accent sounded like "Ann Turner" perhaps this was another one of Harry's little jokes extended from beyond the veil? He most certainly had a great sense of humour, and that little twinkle in his eye, certainly wouldn't have dimmed with his passing, far from it.

If little else added up, out of all this we did agree on one thing at least that Harry was a great man, although we often wonder what he was doing in England at the time of his passing?

Max our Doberman

CHAPTER 11

Foxy footsteps

Pulling the bedroom blinds this particular night, and looking out into the street as you do! I saw what looked like at first glance, a big dog (Alsatian) walking as brazen and bold as you like down the middle of the road! I quietly whispered for Tony to come and see, realizing then that it wasn't a dog, but a large foxy with a beautiful tail (blimey!) must get my eyes tested!

Just then the foxy eyeballed us, (Who you looking at?) And would you believe it strolled over to our front step, and cocked his leg up, the cheeky bugger. One more quick look at us, and then off down the road he strolled! Without a care in the world, we couldn't believe our eyes.

We decided it was best to chuck a bucket of water over our front step to get rid of any aromas (pongs) that might waft across to our neighbours, we were doing this dressed in our night attire (PJs) oblivious to anyone seeing us, although mind you it was quite late, can you imagine our embarrassment if we had been spotted by some curtain twitcher? In the paper the next day the headline could read "Couple seen washing door-step in night-attire" shock horror!

The following morning, when we let Max, our big sloppy Doberman out for his morning toiletries (woof! Woof!) we noticed our side fence was leaning down, on further investigation it was noticed that an animal had actually dug a tunnel into our garden, as you know having read this far, we had placed a chickens wire fence all around our lovely garden in an effort to keep Max away from our fish-pond, as he liked to play with them by dipping his paw in the water! Splash! Splash!

Had this beautiful foxy adopted us? We certainly believed so! The following weeks, months, and years Max would always let us know when foxy was about, he would stand at the back door wanting to be let out, the howling and yapping noise that Max and the foxy used to communicate could be heard all over the neighbourhood, dear me!

Although we fixed the leaning fence we didn't fill in the tunnel, so foxy could come and go as he pleased, we would often put out a knotted bag of Max's food (Tripe, yuk,) for him, which he carried off, we like to think that he was probably taking it back home to his wifey and cubs.

A few years later we moved only a couple of mile up the road, please read on for the amazing outcome about this story! While visiting our friends Erica Saunders, and Ted Wellor many years before we shared a delightful experience with them a mother foxy and her baby cubs had adopted them, and each night about 10.30pm they could be seen walking along the road right up to Erica and Ted's door step to collect their little knotted bag of cats food (yum yum,) and take it off back to their lair, I mention this because it was such an incredible thing to witness.

Getting back to what I was telling you, we moved (were we like gypsies) but only a few miles up the road, we soon settled in and before we knew it the cold, wintry, snowy months were upon us, brrrrr. I believe that first winter there was the coldest we had experienced for years, the snow was very deep in places, and the roads were treacherous like an ice-skating rink, it got so bad that Tony had to leave the car and walk to work about five miles away (poor sausage!)

On his way walking home from night shift he called in to the shop as usual to pick up our daily paper, the snow had been falling heavy, but at least now it had actually stopped as he approached home he could see in the fresh snow footprints, probably that of a cat (large cat,) he was not the only one about this time of the morning, still dark and freezing, as he carried on up the road he noticed that the footprints seemed to be leading to our street, as he turned the corner the footprints could be seen to go right up to our house, he realised then that these were the paw prints of a foxy they went clearly up our drive, to the side of the house, up to our 6 foot wooden gate then just stopped, on opening the side gate the footprints were found again leading right up to our back door.

No nice 6.30am wake-up cup of tea for me that morning, just a very excited hubs (Tony) shaking a sleepy Ann from the depths of her lovely warm slumber, was I having a night-mare? Rubbing sleep from my eyes (yawn) and with my dressing gown half on and half off, Doberman around my leg doing his best to trip me up, waging his little stubbly tail as if he was a good boy, trying at the same time to keep up with Tony as he set off back down the stairs, he was trying to explain to me about the foot-prints but to be honest it wasn't really sinking in, once the back kitchen door was open bbrrrr! I could grasp what he was saying and could see the paw-prints coming from our back gate, which by the way were quickly disappearing under more snow falling, what a wonderful sight, our foxy from our other house had some how tracked us down! We knew it was him without a doubt when Max's howling (woof) was answered by foxy yapping at the end of our garden at that time was overgrown with bushes and trees and resembled a forest so every-night once again it was yummy! Tripe in a knotted bag for him although he always took the food away we never saw him, but could hear him! How privilege we were that foxy had decided to adopt us.

There was one small problem, our neighbours kept two ducks quack, quack, and having heard foxy decided to put poison down in their garden and around their duck pond. We certainly could understand their fear with foxy on the prowl thinking to himself, yummy ducky snacks for dinner, which is natures way after all is said and done!

Max our Doberman

We never did hear his welcoming voice again after that, and less then a years later our dear old faithful friend Max, his health started to decline, he started to go blind, then his back legs started to fail him, eventually the Vet said that there was no more he could do for him, and that we were lucky that we had him as such a loyal companion, for as long as we did, he was thirteen at the time, which is marvellous for a Doberman, and he still loved his grub!

The dreadful day came whilst Mum was visiting us for awhile from London. Tony's Mum was also there, as she had kindly offered to help hack and scythe down our overgrown garden, suddenly Max let out a bloodcurdling howl that tore right through us, my Mum said quietly "Ann he is trying to tell you he's ready to go on his homeward journey homeward journey meaning to the spirit life. I phoned the vets and explained, and asked for a home visit, the vet and the nurse arrived within ten minutes, Max was lying comfortably on his chair (throne) with my arms around him, and I whispered sweet loving words of endeamnent in his ear, as the vet administered the injection that set him free to join foxy and all our spirit family/pets in the life everlasting.

I said a little loving prayer, sending him on his way, thanking him for being a loyal friend to us, the vet, nurse, and both mums bowed their heads in respect as I said my prayer which I thought was very kind of them. With Max now lying peacefully in his chair, his catty friends our family pets gathered round looking on as if to say what a "lazy bones" he is sleeping in the afternoon, meow, meow.

The kettle was put on for a nice cuppa! You can imagine how all three of us were feeling words at that time were not needed, so it was potatoes peeled, veg on, meat in the oven for dinner as Tony would soon be home from work.

Max lying in his chair looked like he was having forty winks, which as he grew older he loved to do, woof woof, sitting beside his chair was the materialised form of foxy, seen clearly by Tony, Mum and I, he was yapping, as if to say I am here to walk my old friend home to the spirit life.

Later on that evening a lovely large hole dug and Max laid to rest right next to his favourite place, the koi-pond. So he could watch those koi as they darted in and out of the lilies and reeds saying to him you can't catch us slow coach ha, ha, gurgle, gurgle, Splash!

Some time later, either side of Max (woof) we placed Sunny, and Tabs two of our treasured family cats (meow meow) and a stone Buddha to set it all off, a few years later when we took some photos of the garden,in its un-finished state, we saw some unusual spirit mists! also a spirit face (eyes) could it be our furry friends Max, Tabs, and Sunny paying a little visit to us? Having a romp and enjoying themselves, we would like to think so!

Ted and Erica Saunders

Spirit activity top left near our Koi pond in Kent

CHAPTER 12

Spiritualist Association of Great Britain
Every now and again we, Tony and I would have a little treat, or as in this case a big, big, one. We would go to the S.A.G.B, to witness the many international mediums that gave fantastic demonstrations, never in my wildest dreams did I think that little old me, might one day be a residential medium at the S.A.G.B and be standing on the platform there, giving out evidential spirit messages, no way!

This particular evening that we had gone along to, there was a demonstration of clairvoyance being held in the Conan Doyle room, the medium taking the demonstration was named Philip Corder.

We were I think, the second communicating link that evening, the messages were coming through so direct and very fast, we were barely able to answer yes! yes! yes! the evidence we were given was excellent, our loved ones had certainly arranged to be there that evening, it seemed for awhile that Philip was having a problem breaking the link, not that Tony and I minded, keep it coming we said, and our loved ones did! It was a bit embarrassing looking around the room, as there must have been well over a hundred people waiting in anticipation for messages from their loved ones, as Philip was ending our messages he asked us if we could meet him in the lounge after the demonstration? Yes, we most certainly could, we heard a big sigh (seriously) coming from the other people, as they realised that they might now at long last get a message!

Can you imagine our excitement and delight at getting the chance to meet this brilliant International medium, who was such a wonderful channel for spirit, we didn't have to sit in the lounge long, before in strolls Philip, this tall, very slight man, he looked different in person, then he did when up on the platform demonstrating, mind you he would, of course! Being a trance medium his guide would have been overshadowing him, almost like a second skin, his eyes would go up as he demonstrated, and you could only see the whites of his eyes, truly amazing!

After a little introduction and chat (spiritual chin-wag,) he invited us over to the residential cottage where he, and the other mediums stayed during their weeks venue, what a truly wonderful evening that was, we shared so many conversations about spiritual events, I think we must have covered most topics, we felt as if we had known each other for a whole life time! Perhaps we had, if you understand my meaning! I can't recall how many times the kettle was put on and to be honest I can't recall either the other people (mediums) coming into the kitchen that night, but I know that they did, because it was a communal kitchen, they were very discreet and so very kind, weren't Tony and I privileged? Towards the end of the conversation Philip tried to give me a heart attack by suggesting that little old me should put in for an "Audition" at the S.A.G.B. I don't think so! But, after many more cups of tea (slurp.) Philips uncanny, convincing manner won me over, and I agreed to at least think about it, was I insane or what? As they say "Nothing ventured, nothing gained," it was 11.30pm now where had all the time gone? Surely the S.A.G.B would be closed, and all the security alarms set, were we here for the night? We didn't know then that the residential (mediums) cottage, which was at the back of the main building and was accessed through a lovely flower garden, had a front door that opened up into a mews, that same lovely flower garden, would in the future be a place that I would sit quietly, and reflect while recharging my inner batteries, after saying our farewells, we started on our homeward journey, reflecting and chatting about our marvellous day so much so that we both cough, cough, suffered from a sore throat (honestly!) For at least a week, what a fantastic day we had and so unexpected! The welcome we received on arriving home from our furry friend's woof, woof, meow. Crikey! You would have thought that we had been away for a year, not just a few hours out of one day! They had been fed, watered, and comforted by their baby-sitter. Alison from next door who always spoilt them babies!

S A G B, Belgrave Square, London

S.A.G.B Audition

Some months later, after thinking long and hard about it. (Tony wouldn't let me forget what Philip had said, yawn!) I somehow mustered up the courage and confidence and decided to put the wheels into motion and apply for an audition (gulp!) At the S.A.G.B, Belgrave Square! It meant obtaining five written references from five different Spiritualist churches or centres. The written references had to include at least five years of service, stating my character, quality of spiritual evidence, and of philosophy given out during the addresses, this was by no means an easy task! What with the postal delays and the church secretaries finding time, as we all know life to-day is so hectic, some of us barely have time to digest our food before we are up and at it again, thinking about it now don't we all seem to have to many commitments, life can some times seem so short and go by in a flash!

Nowadays references could be sent by e-mail, pronto! All done and dusted in two minutes, thank you very much! But back then the poor postie was relied upon more, walking the leather off his boots in the dark dismal, cold and rainy mornings. My patience held out, the references were received and duly sent off to the S.A.G.B., after a short while an appointment was made, and confirmed, for me to take an audition, so there we were Tony and I driving to London S.A.G.B., here we come, my nerves were raw, and my stomach was all over the place, crikey the roads were so busy, on top of that it was windy and chucking it down, my thoughts were no, no! I can't do this lets just turn around now and head for home. As Tony drove the car he was humming away to a CD playing, trying to ignore what was obviously written across my face, cup of tea and biscuit time, he had made a flask up, whatever would I do with out him, so we pulled up into a lay-by drank our tea, and nearly scoffed a whole packet of yummy biscuits. Tony was saying that I would never forgive myself if I turned around now, so in tune with my thoughts; he could read me like a book, without looking at the pages, he must be psychic! Better be careful what I think! My stomach was gurgle! gurgling! I hadn't or couldn't eat breakfast that morning, poor me! We journeyed on into London and at last arrived in Belgrave Square, it took us at least another hour to find an empty parking meter, unfortunately it was about twenty minutes walk away, by the time we got into the S.A.G.B my poor little feet were killing me, ouch!

In through the double doors we went (gulp!) Reporting our arrival at the reception desk, no backing out now, that's the first part over and done with. I was feeling a little relieved now, mind you only a little, hiding in the ladies was always an option open to me (plan-B) we were shown to the tea room for more cups of tea, slurp, with at least six spoonfuls of sugar! We waited there in anticipation, looking up, wide eyed every time some-one peered around the door. Tony was whispering sweet word of encouragement and love to me, trying his hardest to build up my confidence, I could hear the clock as its hands made their way round to 3pm my allotted audition time. The tick-tock-ticking of the clock was in unison with the thud-thump thudding of my heart... .Suddenly the chairing lady (whose name I can't recall) was there explaining the order of the demonstration to me, then we were walking into the packed hall heading towards the platform, my whole body was vibrating with nerves, (to late to run now I suppose?) Completely shot, thinking to myself that I was definitely going to go over (faint!) That was all I needed, falling flat on to my face, then my good friend "Chang" was there beside me his voice calmly saying "be loyal to your inner being (spirit) embrace all opportunities, it is the life's work that you have chosen, this the life of which you live, and all the many different journeys that you take I am with you my little one always we walk together".

The chairing lady introducing me now, all the eyes of the audience staring and smiling up at me, hello! So many people gathered in the hall including the sponsors of the S.A.G.B, the sponsors are the main body of the S.A.G.B people that had spent a life time giving their support to Spiritualism.

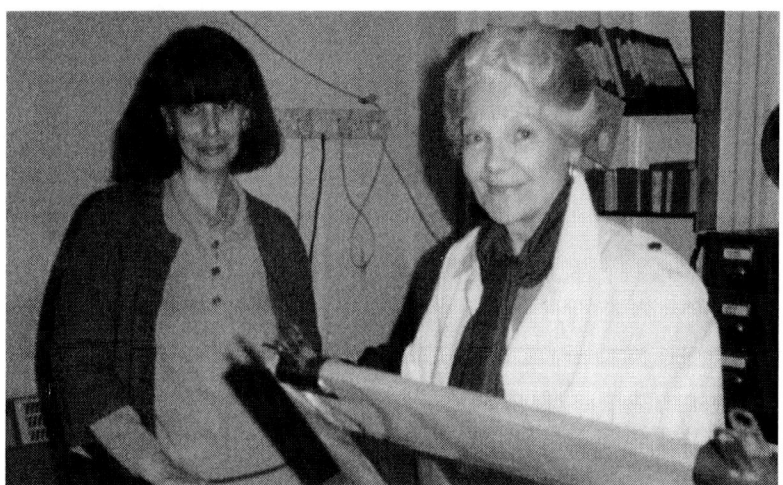

Receptionists at the S A G B

One hour later, where had the time gone? Suddenly I was awake (had I been asleep?) To the thunderous, deafening clapping, ouch, my ears! It took a moment or two for me to adjust my thoughts (vibration) back to the realisation of where I was! The chairing lady was speaking to me but her words were not audible to me at the time, then we were up and she was escorting me out of the Conan Doyle hall. Yes, the very hall that Tony and I had met and witnessed Philip Corders brilliant demonstration.

As I left the hall with the chairing lady, we stopped at the door and I shook the hand of every member of the audience, thanking them for coming

Then it was out the door, ta, ta, in the car, brum! Brum! And on the way home, first chance that I had to let all those pent up emotions free, the tears just flowed and flowed, at the same time asking Tony over and over again, had I let spirit down? Could I have done better? Doubts and more doubts creeping in, I was feeling more of a nervous wreck now then I had felt before the audition, now I had to wait one long month or even longer for the dreaded written results of my audition!

I was quite sure that I had failed, we decided to call in at McDonalds, a rare treat for us, it certainly cheered us up! especially after scoffing those double cheeseburgers with large fries, and milk shake to wash it all down with! Burp! Lovely! This was followed by a nice relaxing evening in front of the box (TV) and the phone switched off and no more discussion about the S.A.G.B and my audition! We spent a lovely evening cuddling our furry friends, meow! Meow! Woof!

The next morning I awoke feeling surprisingly fresh having slept very well, thank you! My only thought about the audition, was that I had given my best, done and dusted! Another day, things to do, places to go!

I could hear the phone ringing, and was hesitating to answer it, but it might be some one in need, so I picked it up. "Hello" surprise! Shock! It was Jean the general mediums booking secretary from the S.A.G.B., straight to the point, yes! Yes! Yes! I had passed the audition, blimey! I was standing up as I was answering the phone, and my legs started to wobble turning to jelly, best sit down quick Ann, passed, had I heard right? I heard myself asking Jean, s-s-stuttering and stumbling over the words, my nerves once again all over the place! I was practically arguing with her, saying to her that I was told the result would come to me in the post in a month! How come you're telling me over the phone?

She explained to me that as she was leaving the S.A.G.B the evening before, she had literally bumped into several of the sponsors, who once a month vet and assess the auditions, and my name came immediately into the conversation, Jean was then told to phone "Ann Turner" first thing in the morning and let her know that she had passed her audition with flying colours, wow! Could she also make sure that she required from "Ann" dates that she would be able to work next month at the S.A.G.B., as you can well imagine I was now all over the place! Tony was in the back ground listening, only hearing half the conversation, but guessing the results by my mannerisms, the kettle was already on the boil, this was defiantly one time I needed a sweet cup of tea slurp! Slurp! Gurgle!

Jean also informed me that it was the first time, in her many years as mediums booking secretary at the S.A.G.B that such a request had been put forward, "unbelievable!" Her words not mine, she then went on to explain the working hours, finances etc; well that was the beginning.

Tony was to say the least immensely happy for me, in my career as a future International S.A.G.B medium, me! Me! Me!

One big hic-cup though was the travelling; I truly didn't mind going on the train to Victoria Station, and then walking the short distance to Belgrave Square, but Tony really didn't like the idea of me travelling on my own on the trains it caused him great concern (old worry guts!) So after much discussion it was decided that I would work at the S.A.G.B once a week until I got used to it, I couldn't wait, yippee!

So once a week Tony would drive me to the S.A.G.B, and as he was on night shifts at the time, this meant that he would arrive home at 6.30am, grab a couple of hours shut-eye zzzzzz, on our sofa, which I had made up into a bed for him the night before! One funny little problem I found was that once I had made the sofa up into a bed for Tony, and then went off to brush my teeth Max our Doberman thought it was his bed and got into it (cheeky Bugger!) Ready for his Mum to kiss him night, night woof! Woof! Get out you bad boy! that's daddies bed! Once I had woken Tony up, (yawn! Yawn! Stretch!) We had our breakfast together, then it was onto the road and off to the S.A.G.B, ready for me to start my exciting working spiritual day 10am-8pm.

After he had dropped me off (kiss-kiss) he then drove over to my Mums house in Willesden, to spend the rest of the day with her which in his words was a rare treat as she loved to spoil him, she got him a large pork chop dinner, followed by a lovely yummy, fresh cream cake, or roly-poly steamed jam pudding and custard, and of course they always caught up on all the gossip yap! Yap! One of Tony's favourite subjects! Then it was off to bed for him to catch up on his, yawn, (much needed) beauty sleep!

After a while it was decided to conserve energies, and cut down on all the travelling (he was Knackered! Poor love!) I started to stay at the S.A.G.B for a five day venue once a month, staying in the residential cottage, which suited us both. I know that Tony didn't mind me being away, he was only to pleased to be shot of me nag! Nag! Nagging him!

We soon settled into a nice little routine, most working days at the S.A.G.B consisted of giving spiritual readings to people that had booked an appointment in advance, the spiritual readings had to be kept to a strict time limit, which at first I found difficult! But with "Chang" nagging in my ear what choice did I have but to get on with it! Poor "Chang" I sometimes wonder how he copes with all my back-chat! but I suppose it's the same as with any new job you either sink or swim, and I took to it like a baby duck to water, mind you one with a rubber ring on, quack! Quack!

The one thing that my friends will say about me, amongst other things, is that I am persistent, and that I have a will of wrought iron, never giving in to failure either spiritually or materially.

Coral Polge

There was during our busy days "Break-times" when we all met up in the mediums room, for a nice refreshing cup of tea or coffee, and a little chat well (gossip) it was at these times that I would sometimes take photos of the other mediums. "Cheese" a comment was made by Coral (Polge) "for your book Ann?" The other nice part of the break-times was that we gave each other nice little spiritual messages, and we didn't have to pay, sometimes for some reason or another our clients (sitters) would cancel their appointments and on one such occasion Coral asked me if I would like to have the reading, yes please! Which was a very real treat indeed, as you probably know she was a very gifted psychic artist, and for her to have a cancellation was rare.

As she sketched, she gave clairvoyant evidential messages:

Coral– do you know Daisy a family link?
Me– yes! my Auntie
Coral– she lived to a great age
Me– yes! she was 96yrs old when she passed
Coral– she lived by the sea
Me– yes! she did
Coral– she speaks of Eastbourne
Me– yes! she retired to Eastbourne
Coral– she lived a very healthy life
Me– yes she did
Coral– swam in the sea, winter and summer
Me– every week until she passed
Coral– I feel that she passed of old age
Me– yes! she simply went to sleep

As she finished sketching Coral passed me the picture, and although my Aunt Daisy had shown herself as a younger woman, I recognised her portrait immediately, amazing! Absolutely! Fantastic! What a truly gifted medium she was, also adding here that I was privileged indeed to have worked with, and personally known all the excellent mediums, of that era!

Anna Noman

Ann and John Cooper
Medium Crystal Healer

Mark Brandige

Now, many years later, and after shifting through a couple of over stuffed draws (memorabilia!) I have managed to find the photographs that I took of all those dear friends and colleges (mediums) in the mediums room at the S.A.G.B all those years ago, blimey! Where's all the years gone? As with everything, changes take place, and all those brilliant mediums have long since moved on to pastures new, and like myself have left the S.A.G.B behind, progressing along their own spiritual pathways, making way for the up and coming younger generation of psychics.

May I say here a big "Thank you" to all those older mediums that may have progressed to the spirit (Higher) life, for not only allowing me to write of them, but for also allowing me to put their photos in my book.

Serving the S.A.G.B brought about many changes for me, meeting people of different cultures, religions, and beliefs, who had travelled far from overseas, arriving at the doors in anticipation, with the one big thought in their hearts, the hope that their loved ones would take this opportunity to make evidential contact with them, proving that there is a life after physical death, all those that entered the building, must have felt the lovely energizing invisible forces of spirit, (so welcoming) that were present there, and probably still are to-day.

Hilda Holyman
Philip Corder
Ray Howden

Philip Corder
Francis, Ann and
Ruby Whitley

I found travelling overseas on my own, a little nerve-racking to say the least (daunting), the biggest distance that I had been on my own was probably about two hundred miles, but this was over a thousand miles or so, Tony would always say "Don't be such a baby" and still does to this day, cheeky, mind you, I did find that his words always seemed to give me the confidence and courage needed, that's why I was able to except many offered venues overseas. Sometimes being met at foreign airports by strangers, who I had only spoken to over the phone, or as in many cases not being met,help! At these times I always thought had I got onto the wrong plane? Had I got the time schedule wrong? Standing there feeling and looking totally lost my eyes popping out of my head (gulp) as they always do when I'm nervous or stressed, poor me! Where's my sun-glasses? Nice deep breaths Ann, in and out, trying to stay calm, calm nothing helps, no,Tony there to hold my hand and tell me everything is going to be ok or even "Changs" voice as a matter of fact more lessons?

I was connecting with so many people spiritually, all of a like-mind, body and soul, trying to prove and give to the best of my ability, the ultimate evidence of spirit life!

Some people say that we as a Spiritualist movement are going backwards have we lost our status? I don't really think so, I have been lucky enough in my short life-time, to have met and shared the true sentiments of Spiritualism with many lovely people all over the world, and not behind closed doors either!, but in Spiritualist churches and centres, large halls and theatres many filled to capacity. Spiritualism is not just away of life but is now a registered religion, we have come a long way on that never ending journey called life! Spirit life! We sure have.

Our good friend "Shozo" has given us (Tony and I) permission to relate to you in his own words his heart felt true spiritual life story

Spirit arm around me after readings in Wales

CHAPTER 13

Letters

Ann Turner and I　by Shozo Takemoto Japan
It was in February 1992 when I first met Ann Turner at the Spiritualist Association of Great Britain (S.A.G.B) in London. In those days I lived in Rochester, a small historic town about 30 miles to the south east of London. I was a visiting professor at the University of London, and I used to go to the university, to take classes three days a week.

This particular day I had no classes, so I travelled up to Victoria Station by train, and walked the short distance to the S.A.G.B arriving there about noon. I had an appointment with a medium at 1pm, and I was waiting for the sitting in the lounge named Lincoln room. No one else was there, then a young lady came in, "Hello" she said, she was dressed in a white track-suit with the brand name of Beneton on the front, I said to her "are you waiting for a sitting too?" No she answered" I am a working medium here" after a short while I asked her if it was possible for me to have one of her business cards, she gave me her card, that was Ann Turner she then left the room bye! Bye! I took a look at her card and noticed that she also lived in Rochester! (coincidence?) Not to far away from my house, perhaps about 15mins walk. I remember that I felt something familiar with her at the time!

After that I went for my appointed sitting and was told about my wife and son and other family members in the spirit world. I was still in a state of half doubt about the messages that I had been given from those in spirit! But I made a promise to myself that I would return to the S.A.G.B to see if I could obtain any further proof (messages) from my family in the world of spirit. I was like a drowning man clutching at a straw!

My family used to be four, my wife, daughter Yukari, son Kiyonori, and myself. I went to the University of Arizona as a Fulbright senior researcher in April 1982. I was planning to take my wife, and my daughter as she was able to enrol at the same university, my son kiyonori was a university student in Tokyo, and was to remain there alone, unfortunately my wife's mother was hospitalized because of cancer, so my wife decided to stay in Tokyo with our son to look after her mother, my daughter and I went as planned to America, the following year in 1983 I went on to teach at the North Carolina State University, my daughter also transferred to there with me. We set up home in Raleigh which is the capital city, in the summer of that year my wife and son came over from Tokyo to spend the summer vacation with us, one big happy family together again! We managed to visit many tourist attractions, and some lovely places of interest we thoroughly enjoyed our sight seeing trips! But this happy summer vacation was to soon end in tragedy, when my wife and son were on their way back to Japan, the airliner KAL 007 on which they were boarded strayed far into soviet (Russian) airspace, and was shot down by a soviet fighter pilot, all the 269 passengers and crew were killed, including my beloved wife and son! My daughter and I returned to Japan after the tragedy, I just couldn't face the harsh reality of it all, and spent nearly every day and night, week after week in my bed like an invalid. I didn't want to be awake, when I was asleep I could escape from this living nightmare, I felt as though I was half dead.

My deep grief and sorrow went on month after month, after 3 years the shadow of this darkness still hung over me, I had been a professor for many years at one of the National Universities in Hokkaido, a northern island of Japan, but I resigned and moved to Tokyo.

In 1992 I was given the chance to be a visiting professor at the University of London; I thought that this would be a good diversion for my mind.

Ann with Shozo in Kent

Shozo's niece visiting us

In the course of time, when I die, my daughter Yukari will be on her own in this world and I hoped that this would be an appropriate time for her to experience living alone without close family members, so I left Japan on my own!

My appointment at the University of London was for one year, from the 1st of April 1991 to the 31st of March 1992, my classes kept me very busy for the first six months, plus on my days off I was enjoying travelling around England, and on Sundays I would go to church and study the bible, in February of 1992 I started to visit the S.A.G.B in London, and it was about this time that I first met "Ann Turner"

On the 11th of February, I went to the S.A.G.B again, this day was the anniversary of my brothers death! I made an appointment with Ann Turner for the first time, and as I sat face to face with her, (although I hadn't told her anything about myself) I wondered if she would remember me form the Lincoln room a few days before? She knew nothing about my family, or the fact that I was from Japan and living temporarily in Rochester, Kent!

Ann Turner said a small prayer asking for guidance, and then started speaking to me without asking any questions at all and a miracle happened in that small room, my son Kiyonori "appeared" in front of me, I was able to have a miraculous family reunion with the help of Ann Turner my heart swelled up, I was struck by such deep emotion, I was almost weeping in gratitude, as soon as I returned home I wrote the following letter to my daughter in Tokyo to tell her of this miraculous reunion! On this particular day I made an appointment for a sitting at the S.A.G.B in London. The medium was sensitive enough to have an insight into another world; her name was Ann Turner, she was able to speak with your mother and brother in the spiritual world, and informed me that Kiyonori was standing in front of me, looking very moved!

I met Ann Turner in her sitting room for the first time, and I sat in front of her without saying a word, so Ann Turner didn't know anything about me, our family, or the incident this is what she said. The young man that stands in front of you is your son, he is about 5ft 8in tall, and looks very intelligent. Yes! He was about that tall, but I stayed silent as I sat in front of her, she went on, your son is saying his name is Kiyuoni or Kiyohni? She repeated it again trying to pronounce it correctly, Kiyhoni? Kooyoney? I was very startled by the sound of the name that she was trying so hard to pronounce, she must be trying to say Kiyonori, no other name would sound like this, just to make doubly sure I asked Ann Turner the following question is it an English name?

No it is not she replied, it sounds foreign to my ear, certainly the name of Kiyonori would not be easy for an English lady to hear so I ventured to ask her could it be Kiyonori? Yes, it is Kiyonori, he is saying his name is Kiyonori!

It was truly amazing to be told Kiyonori's name in this way, I thought it was so unbelievable; I was concerned that my letter would have an effect on my daughter, I tried to hold my emotions and write as dispassionately as possible, but I was finding it hard to control my loudly throbbing heart! I had been in agony and despair for so long now, month after month for many years and now I knew that I was going to overcome this hardship at last the hardest part of the tragedy was starting to fade.

The letter to my daughter continued; also Ann Turner said, your son says that you have a scar on your left foot! By this time I was answering her, and informed her that I did not have a scar on my left foot! But she was undaunted, saying you must have this scar, it might be almost faded, but you must have this scar, try to find it!

Ann Turner must be an excellent Spiritualist medium but I knew myself better then she did, and I positively declared that I did not have a scar on my left foot, and I was a little dismayed at this "incorrectness" On the way back to Victoria Station, however I suddenly realised that as a child I was burnt on my right foot, and as it was quite serious I still have a scar on my right foot! The word scar also means mark or burn, which I certainly do have and from where Kiyonori was standing in front of me my left foot would have been seen as my right foot! It really was Kiyonori standing in front of me at the time as Ann Turner had said, it was quite a revelation to me, and I was greatly moved.

Three days later I made an appointment to see Ann Turner again at the S.A.G.B I wanted to be sure that it was not a made up story, or just her imagination. I wanted to be confident that my beloved wife and son were alive as many times as I could.

Ann Turner started talking in the same way as before, she talked about my brother and my wife, she delivered messages from the spirit world in away that carried firm and honest conviction.

After listening to her for awhile I said, may I ask you questions? Yes! Three days ago you told me that I had a scar on my right foot, that message turned out to be correct, could you tell me who told you of this? Ann Turner replied, your father did! No, not your father, it was your son! My father also knew, when he was alive that I had this scar so if she had said your father did, it would not have been to wide of the mark, but she properly pointed out my son!

I went on to ask, is my son here in this room? Yes he is here now, your wife is also here with other family members!

I went on to say, my son can speak English, can you ask him in what year he passed away? This may seem a very crossed grained way of asking a question, but as she knew nothing about my family or the incident it would be impossible for an unacquainted person to know when a person was killed,

But Ann Turner replied without hesitation 1973 no 1983 was an especially sad year for you, this year is close to your heart! She then continued I can see a vehicle moving very fast, suddenly it is destroyed so suddenly that all was in confusion, he didn't understand what had happened he saw his own body.

Ann Turner went on to say much more about the incident, but I would rather not repeat the details here, all I can say is that the messages were very much to the point and I was totally convinced that my son was actually in the room, and communicating with us on that day!

I left England at the end of March 1992, even after returning to Japan I have kept in touch with Ann Turner, and with her help, and special gift I have been able to communicate with my son Kiyonori each year on his birthday.

The 1st of September is the day of the incident, and each year on this day for the last 19 yrs Kiyonori's friends have visited us, to pay tribute to the memory of him and his mother, they will probably come again this year to listen to the messages from Kiyonori, to share this special time with us!

The following is one of the special spiritual communications between the two worlds which took place on the 5th of June 02

....

Dear Kiyonori,

Today is your 38th birthday, and I would like to say "Happy Birthday" to you Kiyonori with all my heart. I am now 70yrs old and I am always very thankful that you are my son, and have been for the last 38yrs I still vividly remember your phone-call from Kennedy International Airport in 1983. That was your last call and I sensed in your tone of voice something uneasy and frightening.

After many years of agony and despair I can now understand what it was. I must first of all apologise for my ignorance and arrogance that finally lead you and your mother to the fatal journey. I have written a book with the title of; Beyond the world of Life and Death, it will go on sale in August of this year. The book is dedicated to you and your mother, I hope you get to read it; also I am planning to publish another book, which includes your essays on linguistics. This is my last year at school before retirement and I feel obligated to do what I ought to do within this year.

Your sister Yukari is fine, she is doing voluntary work to help the needy people in the neighbourhood, as you know she has been married nearly eight years now, but still does not have a baby! She seems to be suffering and I pray every day that God will bless her with a child, this is the only concern that we have at present, and everything else is fine. I understand that you are doing some school work in your world, please let me know how your studies are going, also I would be pleased to hear anything about your life and the people around you, how is your mother, and your grandparents? I know that in the future I will see you and other family members and don't feel lonely even living here alone. I feel you are always here with me.

I am very proud of you Kiyonori. You are a warm hearted and intelligent son; I do hope that everything is fine with you and your mother. I pray that Gods light will always be with you both, I am looking forward to hearing from you before to long

　　　　　From your father

　　　　　...

Dear Father,

Thank you father for your Birthday Greetings, I received it with a very open and full happy heart, although a little reminder that I am truly getting older, well mature, I can still be a little conceited! Anniversaries are so special never to be forgotten. You would have felt our presence on your 70th birthday wishing you a very happy day. Anniversaries are proof of ones life growth and communication, a time to share with all those we love dearly, and I love you so my dear father.

It was such along time ago that our last conversation took place in the physical sense that is. Please father forgive my attitude, let my arms embrace you, we have certainly moved forward, and learnt so much over the past 17yrs, much understanding and knowledge we have shared and required which can never be taken or removed from our memory. Many happy times, moments to call upon, when feeling a little sad or lonely.

Do you still have my little clock? Tick! Tock! I speak to you my father with much pride and gratitude for being your son, know that we do have freedom of personal choice and responsibility of ones family and yes! friends a love that is certainly very special, never can it be severed it is in ones heart, in Gods truth, spirit within.

Congratulations on your forthcoming retirement and the many years of happy most fulfilling work that you have done. More time for you father to spend putting your own secret dreams into reality and you do have quite a few don't you? More people to meet, places to visit and most of all books to write what an hectic time you are in for, not sitting around on your bottom

Your book, *Beyond the World of Life and Death* certainly places our two worlds together; always do that of which your heart inspires you. People need to read your wisdom and comforting words to know of our world and life of spirit. Knowledge will grow through understanding of writings such as yours father, filling the gap of our two worlds, eventually putting an end finally of fear and superstition, bringing us all closer together, hence removing so much pain and suffering that grief brings, death being no more then simply a step into another dimension with harmony in ones heart.

Much love to my sister Yukari, my sister is so sensitive, using that special gift working with people, helping them in their moments of need, advising talking to them with her quietly controlled mannerism. Please father, give her a big embarrassing cuddle from me, her big brother! she will understand, regards to her husband, my brother in-law shake his hand strongly from me, tell him to celebrate that special anniversary in March, enjoy be happy, I am, and we are all so pleased that he joined our family.

Mother wishes to speak to you father.

....

My dear husband, you have become a worrying man in your older age, do not deny this! You are still so modest saying little and thinking to much. Yukari is fine; she enjoys her work as you know. It takes her mind off her own problems. Be a little more stronger for her my husband for she senses your concern and worry. Ask her to drink 2 litres of water per day religiously; I know that this will not please her, water not being one of her favourite drinks; however this will do her good giving her physical body equal balance and will help to assist, to keep her system clean.

I have seen her contentment of recent years; tell her we are all in Gods hands. Whatever his great and mighty plan and will, it will be when the time is correct for the birth of that bundle of joy. There will be many happy years shared, many happy years shared together.

I am never far away from you my daughter and know your feelings on this matter, slow down a little, Rome wasn't built in a day! Why all that rushing? Whatever am I going to do with you, listen to your husband with both ears! With much affection and love, your mother.

I am truly proud of you, and for you my husband, live your life to the full for it is good, all family members give their love to you in abundance. They do draw close and keep their eyes on you at all times, helping when they can my husband, but not interfering into your life too much, simply being near to you. Feel us! Sense us and hear all our little messages directly from our son for we place them into your mind at all times.

When you have a special reunion my husband and play the tape machine and these messages feel our love and energies like an envelope enclosing you, all being there all around you, our family is such a family unit that we are. We look forward to that special reunion when our worlds are bought together by the love we share. I love you my husband, always and forever your wife.

As you know father I am studying spirit communication, how many marks out of ten do you give your son? Your answer will tell me, how well my studies are going and doing. Please confirm my laughing father and send your answer directly to me via your thought.

Our medium Ann and channel we use most gratifying for this communication as you know has such a draining effect on her energies which are getting very low. So I will say, we will all say Bye! Bye for now and thank you father, for being my father. I love you

from your son Kiyonori

....

Just a little note here to mention that when Shozo left England to return home to Japan, after his one year stay (April 1991- March 1992) as a visiting professor at the University of London, the actual date of his return was 31st of March which coincidently is my birthday, and also Hydesville day in the modem Spiritualist calendar. I would also like to write here that Shozo, his family, and us (Tony and I) have become firm friends, he has on several occasions over the years (when in England) visited our home for lovely spiritual conversations, tea and biscuits, we always exchange Christmas cards, and memorabilia each year and I pray that the communicating link, that exists between our two worlds, which I have been privileged to serve as a channel, (And I give a heart warming "thank you" to spirit life) continue for the many years to come.

134

Please see photo of Shozo and I, taken in our front garden, when we lived in Rochester about nine years ago.

The following is a selection of letters that have been received over the years.

Sandy from Australia
I met Sandy (at the S.A.G.B) a young English woman, now living in Australia, the following is a letter that I received from her some years ago, confirming spirit evidence.

Her letter

In April 1984 I spent all day waiting for a phone call from Ruth, my best friend, to say she was back from her holiday (a family holiday to France) I had been intending to accompany her, but at the last minute I pulled out due to exam revision pressure.

Then the newsflash came on the television, their car had been involved in a crash, and the whole family had died, her mum, dad, sister Rachael 1 1yrs old and Ruth 16yrs old. Two men had allegedly been test driving a fast car, and had ploughed into the back of their vehicle whilst it was parked on the hard shoulder of the French high-way. The car spontaneously crumpled and burst into flames!

The grief and shock of losing my best friend and the realisation that I had narrowly missed an early death, took along time to come to terms with. The empty desk next to me at school, was a reflection of the emptiness I felt inside. The school memorial service, and the four different sized coffins lined up at the funeral, are lasting images I can still visualize to-day.

Ann Turner steps in 8 years later
In July of 1992 a group of friends persuaded me to accompany them to the S.A.G.B in London. I had always been intrigued by Spiritualism and the supernatural and this visit would change my life forever.

As we waited for the clairvoyant demonstration to begin, butterflies danced around in my tummy, a mixture of excitement and nervousness.

Ann Turner (medium) entered the Oliver Lodge hall and stepped up onto the platform, she said a lovely opening prayer, and started talking saying how excited the spirits were about the afternoon. She had many human and animal friends and relatives equally expectant as we were! When she started describing a young lady, who showed herself firstly with long dark hair to her waist, and then sporting a short spiky style I raised my hand, Ruth had made this brave and striking image change shortly before her holiday, and was very proud of it.

Once I had claimed her, Ann began to contort in intense pain all over her body and stated that she was burning, at this moment my tears started to flow but instantaneously Ann said she felt okay! And the pain was gone at this point I asked if she was alright? Ann replied "Yes, and she wants you to move on, and get on with living your life and have fun!" In fact Ruth's parting words to me were "Have fun" as she gave me a big wave and smile, before setting off on her holiday 8 years before.

Ann then mentioned a little tortoiseshell cat, which I didn't claim because I never actually owned one myself, I didn't realise that because I had known and dearly loved a friends cat which had disappeared it would come to me! I never stopped looking for Sukey when she failed to return home one day so "Thank you" for saying hello little kitten.

Sandy and family, Australia

Jasmine with spirit orb on her skirt

The Plumbers Arms

We all met Ann again a week later, and went to a small London pub, called the Plumbers Arms, on walking into the pub I asked if there was an upstairs (which is unusual) but there was, and we all climbed a narrow staircase to a private lounge. Ann inform us that we were frequently being checked on by a lady, who was dressed in a white gown, she wore a cap on her head, and was carrying a candle!

When we were leaving I enquired to the landlord about the history of the pub, he pointed out a poster in a frame on the downstairs wall which detailed some pub history, the pub was very old and used to be split unto two bars, one bar for the wealthy, and one bar for the poor, one was upstairs and one was downstairs, there was also a newspaper cutting mounted on another wall which detailed this mystery of a man who murdered his house-keeper, and then disappeared himself (I wonder if this was the spirit lady that Ann had seen upstairs?) It obviously has a lot of history.

Soon Ruth was coming through and asked Ann to "Budge over" (move over) so that she could sit next to me. Ruth then elaborated on her passing which is very private and close to my heart, I would rather not mention her words. Ruth then mentioned that she had seen me crying, and unable to sleep, she just wanted me to know that she is still very close.

Just knowing that my relatives and friends are all safe, happy and pain free is a priceless gift of peace that Ann Turner has given to me.
I admire Ann Turner the medium, and I love Ann Turner my friend!

Another letter from Sandy in Australia
Dear Ann and Tony,

Well I don't know how I found it, but I have just located the letter that you sent me in October 1996, which gave me life changing news of Jasmine's future birth. The letter had become separated from my stash of very important sentimental memorabilia. So "Thank you" for any spirit help that made me look in that drawer in the garage!

Earlier in 1996, I had a miscarriage at 12 weeks, Matt (my son) was a very busy 2 year old, and I was very home-sick for England.

Your letter read; "how about a baby girl, and little sister for Matthew, the month of March comes to me, also the 27th 5lb 6oz just a little message of encouragement, please try not to be to apprehensive, you will hold that bundle of joy I promise, goodness me you will have both hands legs and everything else filled, then wherever will you find the time to write even a few lines to Ann,such happy times ahead!"

So with these wonderful words of encouragement I kept trying for Jasmine, in March 1997 Mum and Dad came over to Australia for a months holiday, and Matthew and I decided to go home with them for a six week holiday, when we visited and stayed with you for a few days in Rochester (in late May early June) as Matthew and I were on your doorstep before entering your home you said "So are you, you know? And I said "No" and you replied "Well they must be getting you ready".

On arriving back in Australia, and within the first few days of my return I fell pregnant. I was rather worried during the pregnancy, after the experience of both a premature baby and a miscarriage, but all went well!

Jasmine was due at the end of March 1998, she decided that she liked it so much in my tummy that she would rather stay there and on the 2nd of April I was booked in to have an induction at 7.30am, but she had other ideas and arrived very quickly at 4.56am (I awoke at 3am with a contraction, made a hot drink, enjoyed it between contractions, waited until 3.20am then woke Adam and got to the hospital at 3.30am) her birth weight was 8lb 5.5oz, you also sent me another letter of congratulations, just before she was born informing me of a strawberry birth mark on the back of her neck, this was absolutely correct!

Tony and I are still very much in contact with Sandy, husband Adam and the children, Matthew and Jasmine; we keep in constant contact by e-mail, phone and text messages.

A letter from Brenda…London
My name is Brenda, and I went to the headquarters of the Spiritualist Association of Great Britain (S.A.G.B) on Monday the 12th January, and had a half hour sitting at 2.30pm with Ann Turner, a natural born Spiritualist medium, we had never met prior to this sitting.

I was overwhelmed at the accuracy of the information that Ann was able to give me. Firstly I was given the name "George" this is the name of my Grandfather (deceased) and my natural father. Ann then talked of my son in the spirit world, to my knowledge I have only ever been pregnant twice I would also like to add that after my sitting with Ann I stayed on at the centre, and went to a demonstration where another medium came to me and told me exactly the same thing!

Ann then went on to tell me that there was a split in a love relationship, and that I was now separated from that person, she gave me the name of "David" this is the name of the father of my children we are now separated. Ann also told me she could see another person in my life, she said he is dark, and gave me the month of November, my present husband is West Indian and born in the month of November.

Ann went on to tell me that my deceased Grandfather is looking after my spirit son, who is grown up now. Ann also gave me the name of "Barry" this is the name of one of my brothers. Ann also gave me the letter "S" which is the initial of my youngest daughter, and told me that my eldest daughter would be 17 this year, she is in fact 17 in September of this year.

The sitting was only 30mins long, and I feel sure that there is no way possible for Ann to have given all the personal details, names especially if she is not truly gifted as a spiritual medium. I will be going to meet Ann again for a full reading!

God bless you Ann

Brenda.

A letter from Karen…Ashford

Dear Ann,

Perhaps you will recall me and my Mum, from a sitting that we had with you on the 11th May at 2pm. I feel I must write and thank you for a most wonderful hour, there was such a vitality and energy that we felt uplifted for days following, in fact we found it very difficult to leave. This wasn't due to wanting prolonged contact with our spirit family members, but had more to do with you! We felt a rapport, and would have loved to have stayed longer to talk with you!

Both Mum and I would welcome an opportunity to meet you again "Outside business" as it were, if you feel the same please write or telephone, if however you would rather not, for any reason, don't worry we will understand and be content!

My father certainly made his self known to Mum and I, however many of the messages that my father gave are of a personal nature, which we would rather not disclose.

The "Tall well-dressed lady, with hat and gloves on" who we couldn't place her during the sitting, when you spoke of her, I felt she was my paternal grandmother, but couldn't quite connect the description, going home my Mum, confirmed that is who she was!

Also you gave us "Southend" and I thought I knew the connection, but was later to discover I was mistaken. However at 11pm that evening my husband and I were still awaiting the return of our 16yr old son, who had not come home for the evening meal. He arrived home apologising madly because he had been to "Southend" with a friend, we did laugh! I actually found it rather comforting to know that he is being "Overseen" as this life of his seems to be one of first-hand experience in many areas, which has caused him and the family many trails, tribulations and opportunities for learning. It is all very well understanding "Why" but it can still leave us quite frazzled at times.

I hope these couple of up-dates are of interest, I thank you once again for an uplifting and evidential spiritual sitting. Take good care.

Kindest regards
Karen.

A letter from Thelma...Falmouth Cornwall
Dear Ann,

I was so delighted to meet you on the 11th of Jan; it seemed to me as if we were not strangers to each other, I don't know how that could be?

When my husband John said that he wanted to go to the boat show at Earls Court, I said that I would go with him, so I phoned up Belgrave Square (S.A.G.B) and made two appointments at once. This done, I waited for a suitable time when I was alone in the house and unlikely to be disturbed, I spoke out loudly to the air. To my son Colin who had recently passed. I said "Colin, listen, I am going to try for a contact with you on Monday and Tuesday, if I were you I would ask Dad (that is my father) to bring you, as he has come to me so often, and you are quite new to spirit life! That is exactly what happened, at that wonderful spiritual sitting that I had with you Ann. You gave me an anniversary for December and you mentioned the year 1990 and the number 35 you also added "I have a very tall gentleman about six foot odd, he is telling me that he is your father he looks a very strong man, and he has a younger male with him, his grandson, you also mentioned the name of Colin, the year of 1946- 1949, I dissolved into tears of joy at the contact, and for a moment or two words failed me! My father was no ordinary man; he stood 6ft 2in in his socks, and his spirit more then matched his physical body in strength, if he were in charge of a situation, as he always was, there would be nothing to worry about! He passed over in 1949. Our youngest son Colin died on the 12th Dec 1990 three days after his 35th birthday, all of the messages were so correct!

I myself had a very brief contact with my son about a year after his passing, it happened one morning at 5am, I was not asleep, but very drowsy we had our arms around each other, and he said "I've got a new suit of clothes on now" that was all, there were other messages given at the time, but the most important contact for me was the evidence given

concerning my son Colin, I can not thank you enough Ann, and hopefully we will be able to return to see you again in the not to distant future.
With love from
Thelma

Whilst searching amongst my memorabilia on the 14th Feb 2007, for this book I came across this letter, and with this letter was a phone number that had the old digit system, I had no sooner read this lovely heart felt letter, then I rang the operator and obtained the correct digit (code) then I rang the phone number, a gentleman answered the phone, hesitantly I asked if I could speak to Thelma, the gentleman was her husband John and he notified me that his wife Thelma had passed on the 1st of Aug 1998, he then asked who I was, I then went on to explain I was Ann Turner and I had given Thelma a reading at the S.A.G.B many years ago. I explained about the letter and asked his permission to include his wife's lovely letter in my book he asked me if I would kindly read the letter to him, which I did! The whole of the conversation was extremely emotional, he said to me that "my wife as already given you permission by inspiring you to find the letter" before I rang off I promised to send him a copy of our book if and when we finish it, or when it is published.

A letter from Evie...Middlesex
Dear Ann,
Ed and I met you at the S.A.G.B many years ago. Ed is an American friend of ours, and although I can not remember any of the messages given by you at the S.A.G.B 1hr double sitting, which Ed and I shared, I can however recall the evening of that sitting, when you had finished your days spiritual work, you came to my home in Middlesex, where I introduced you to my husband Pete, he was in another room when the special event took place, we shared the most amazing spirit inspired evening that we have ever witnessed in our lives, this proved to be one of the most enlightening validations I have ever had.

As "Chang" your good friend and guide began speaking through you, he appeared before our very eyes in ectoplasm form, an experience I had never had before, or since. It was so clear and vivid, Ed was shocked and unable to make sense of it for a while! I was mesmerised and excited that such physical medium-ship should be occurring in my home. Had I had any doubts about the existence of the Spirit World, which I've never had, that was a definite validation.

Not all such validation is on such a scale as previously mentioned, but to each person their personal validation means so much. The following is another letter that Evie sent to me, recounting two of her own personal spiritual experiences;

Dear Ann,

These are just two of the many spirit validations that I have received over the years, the first concerns the umbrella that I left on my ottoman. Some day's later I went to get it and it was no-where to be found, I looked everywhere but was unable to find it, very strange! Because I know that was the place I put it, any way a week later it mysteriously appeared back on top of the ottoman exactly where I had placed it! Strange but true!

The second validation that I received was to do with my mother. Her favourite flower was the rose of peace, and roses were very special to her. On this occasion I was at home and left the lounge to go to my bedroom stepping from the hall into the bedroom there was an overpowering smell of roses! But stepping back into the hall, there was no smell of roses! I called to my husband Pete and asked him to repeat my movements, but did not say why, his experience was incredibly the same as my own!

Over the years flower scents have been around me many times, just letting me know that my mother is there.

God bless you

Ann Evie

A letter from Sandie… Kent

I have known Ann and Tony for many years, in my roll as president of the Tenterden Spiritualist Church, they have demonstrated their gifts of clairvoyance and psychic art for us many times, they always bring much love and laughter, as well as closure where needed, for those in the congregation, when they decided to move to Wales it was a great loss not only to the churches that they served, but to Kent as a whole. I feel very honoured to still have contact with them.

About 18 months ago Ann and Tony completed a series of invited spiritual venues, in and around Kent, and we were lucky enough to receive a demonstration at our church. At that time unbeknown to them I had been asking spirit for lots of help, guidance and the answer to a specific question, I wanted to receive peace of mind, without going into too much detail, I had been going through a lot of emotional turmoil at home, and in my marriage.

It started about 2-3yrs prior to their visit, and although I had known Ann and Tony for some time, it was always on a professional level, never on a personal one, so they were completely unaware of my dilemma!

It all started with the very sudden death of my husband's father which left a lot of shock, anger, and sadness within the family, my husband put himself more into his work, and spare time activities, this left very little time for my son and I. He would often come home late saying he was out walking or running etc, which eventually caused rows and doubts within our relationship.

I know many mediums through my work at the church, but never felt as though they were the right ones to give me the answers I so needed, so when Ann and Tony offered to give me a reading over the telephone, a little voice in my head told me "They are the ones" and I asked Ann if I could contact them, it was agreed, but unfortunately when the allotted time came around I had to cancel, another date was made, but unfortunately this time they had to cancel! Third time lucky! I eventually had my reading in the January of 2006.

When I rang Tony answered, he began the reading almost immediately (Ann was in another room, and knew nothing of his reading to me!) Tony gave me a lot of names, and evidential messages from people who have passed over, this amazing reading went on for at least half an hour, then Ann came onto the phone, and started her reading, she immediately picked up on my emotional problems and the anguish over my marriage. Through her reading she actually gave me the answers, I was so desperate to hear. She told me my husband loved me, and that he had always been loyal and faithful to me, and our marriage! I was so overjoyed that tears began to flow immediately. I then went on to tell her of my fears and doubts and how much it was tearing me apart! She was quite shocked and said I never showed it. Ann also picked up on my late father-in-law and passed me messages from him, then my mother came through and this was so emotional, not only for me, but also for Ann. We were both in tears it was such a beautiful reading, and knowing that my loved ones in the spirit world are there for me gave me such upliftment and encouragement this to me was an amazing feeling, and bought to a close 3yrs of hurt, distrust and torment with the words, "He is faithful to you"

Ann and Tony helped me more then they could ever know, and I know that God and spirit sent them to my church in order for me to ask for that wonderful reading, which gave me the answers to all my questions! I have been able to move on with my life and rebuild my marriage since that reading and I am now very secure and happy once more.

Thank you Ann and Tony for all you did for me, and the many others you and your spirit guides help.

God bless you both.

Love Sandie X

Letters from Patsy, Paul and family...Bethersden, Kent

Dear Ann and Tony,

I have always, for many years been interested in the psychic/spiritual side of life, but it wasn't until recently, after my Mum died, that I attended a Spiritualist church with my younger sister for the first time. Ann and Tony were taking the service, at the meeting I seemed to feel very close to Ann although I had never met her before! I watched Ann for awhile, giving out spiritual messages to people in the congregation, but was taken totally by surprise when she started to describe a lady, who had lots of badges, a walking stick, and no teeth in! My Mum collected badges, and if anyone in our family went on holiday, she would always ask them to bring her back a badges, she also walked with a stick, and had no teeth. Ann then mentioned a "Bob" who was standing with my Mum, this could only be my brother Bob who had died some 12yrs earlier.

After that church meeting I spoke to Ann and Tony and arranged for them to come to my home which they kindly did! at a later date!

During this visit, many wonderful spirit messages were given and received to both myself and my family my Mum also came through again, and said I used to boss her about, (which I did!) she now realised that she needed it, that I was a good girl, (I still am!) and that she would at some point come and visit me in my dreams Ann said Mum was talking about my bad back... (I had injured it in a bad car crash!) Ann then went on to mention Ron (My Dad) who had passed over about 40yrs ago. I found the visit by Ann and Tony a great comfort and would like to thank them so very much.

Love
  Patsy

Whilst talking to Patsy on the phone on the 14th Feb.2003 and discussing the bad crash that she was involved in, a gentleman named Ron (Her Dad) drew close to us, and explained that he talked to Paul (Husband) after the horrific crash to help him regain consciousness, and tried to pull open the car door! to help Patsy and Paul's friends get out, the car had hit the crash barrier turned over twice and was upside-down in a ditch half filled with water, on Romney Marsh, when everyone was out of the car only the wheels could be seen! This crash happened in 1993.

Husband Paul's letter
When Ann and Tony came to our home, it was my first meeting of any kind with a Spiritualist medium, or anyone involved in this kind of activity.

I had read books, and watched TV programs about this kind of thing and although I am not sceptical, because there is just too much evidence around just to dismiss it out of hand, I was wary about being involved in the evening's proceedings. However my wife was very interested and had been for many years, and after seeing Ann and Tony at a local Spiritualist church decided to invite them to our home, as she had recently lost her mother. I decided to sit in on the evening with my wife, her sister, one of her friends, and our daughter, just to observe or so I thought!

After some general talk Ann started the readings and turning to me said that she had a gentleman who couldn't wait to give me a message! This was the last thing that I had expected. Ann then went on to describe my Dad saying that he had been waiting for such a long time, to give me the message simply that he "Loved me" and was very "Proud" of me. My Dad was a very quiet man and not one to show his true feelings, so to hear this was unexpected and did bring tears to my eyes. I think it must have taken a lot for him to come through and say that to me!

Ann then went on to say that standing behind my Dad was a small rounded lady, the description she gave fitted my Mum, who owing to my Dad being quiet was the more dominant one in their married life together, so I think that it probably surprised Mum that Dad was so eager to talk that night. Ann said that a lady named Babs (My sister) didn't cope with the passing of Mum to well. It was so nice to hear that they were back together again, as Dad died before Mum and her whole life was Dad.

My heart felt thanks to Ann and Tony for Dads messages it meant a lot.
Thank you
Paul

Daughter Lisa's letter
One Tuesday evening, my Mum arranged for a Spiritualist medium to come to our home and talk with us, her name was Ann Turner, I was a

bit worried at first because I didn't know what to expect as I have never attended one of these meetings before.

When Ann came to me, I was very nervous, but the first thing she said was that "Your grandfather is standing by you" as soon as she told me this the whole meeting felt safe and I was no longer worried! I just wanted her to carry on with the messages Ann mentioned a close friend of mine with family problems, she said to tell my friend it was gong to turn out alright, this is true as my friend is planning to be reunited with her Mum after 3yrs Ann also talked about some money left over from Christmas that I hadn't spent she said that I should go and spend it and whatever I bought would be from my grandma! This was quite moving as me and my Nan who as passed away, had been saving 20ps months before Christmas, and we had planned to spend them together when Christmas was over, sometimes I do hear my Nan talk to me like the other day, about the 20ps she told me to take some! I'm not worried about my Nan talking to me I find it reassuring.

Well thank you Ann I found the reading comforting.

     Lisa   (aged 14yrs)

Following this lovely spiritual readings evening at Patsy and Paul's home she sent me a letter containing some of her own personal spiritual experiences:

(1)

My first spiritual experience was when I was 5yrs old; my Mum Lizzy brought my new born sister (Lizzy) home from hospital and she shared my bedroom and it was at this time that I used to wake up and see a woman standing by lizzy's cot staring down at her, this went on for several weeks until one day she just stopped coming. Time went by and our family moved home a short distance away. One day about ten years later the local vicar came round to ask us if we had encountered any problems in our previous home? It was now occupied by a family with a new born baby, and the lady was appearing again! I heard that the vicar went around and conducted an exorcism and as far as I know that put an end to the problem!

(2)

When I was about 9yrs old I remember walking up the stairs, as I got near to the top I saw boots that belonged to my neighbours boy in front of me, as I stared at them they faded away. I learned later that he had been tragically killed at work!

(3)

When I was 18yrs old my dad died after a long illness, I remember 2-3 weeks later waking up one night, and seeing him standing near my bed. I screamed out with shock and he then walked through my bedroom wall!

(4)

As I have said previously I first met Ann at a Spiritualist church, where she and Tony were taking the service, and I managed to arrange for them to come to my home for a readings evening with a few of my family. It was at this meeting that Ann first met my 14yr old daughter Lisa, she told her that she saw her with horses and that she had a talent for hairdressing. Since then my daughter has indeed had a lot to do with horses, and as actually won a few ribbons. Now at the age of 18yrs she is running the local hairdressing salon and is very much in demand by her customers.

During this meeting Ann also went to my sister (Lizzy) and described her friends husband who had been killed in a tragic car accident, she described the car, what happened, and how he died, it was at this point that Ann had to stop as she was feeling his actual moment of his death!

(5)

Two and a half years ago the biggest blow to my life occurred, my eldest daughter Helen died. Helen died suddenly at home, she was badly handicapped but lived at home with us, and her death was devastating. Not long after this I was talking to Ann on the phone. (Ann and Tony had moved to Wales by this time), we had quite a long chat then said our goodbyes, a few moments later Ann phoned back and told me that while we were talking about Helen a large red cross had appeared in the sky, and Ann was of the opinion that it was a sign from Helen as she was a very special girl. Tony put it onto disc, and sent it immediately to us.

We received it coincidently one hour before our very special daughter's funeral, held on the 3rd of Aug 04, my husband and I and all family members were gathered in the sitting room, we watched it in anticipation momentarily, and we all agreed that it was a message from Helen (Oakey), her family nick-name, "Everything is going to be alright Mum and Dad". It was a lovely feeling to know with certainty that Helen was still close and keeping her eye on us, Ann and I continue to keep in touch to this day, and she has been a great comfort to me, giving me lots of little messages from my loved ones in spirit, messages about things that she had no prior knowledge of, Ann and Tony are two of the most loving and genuine people you could hope to meet and I feel privileged to know them!

Patsy   XXX

Patsy and Paul's daughter Helen's
cross in Wales

Helen (Oakey)

Tony's Psychic Art

As I have told you Tony and I have taken clairvoyant/psychic art demonstrations all over the country for many years Crikey! Makes us feel old when I think back that far! After the psychic art demonstrations some people come up to us afterwards, for a little chat, and like to confirm that the portraits they have received of their loved ones are a very close likeness.

Some of these lovely people ask for our address, so they can send us photographic proof that their loved ones were actually there in person, even after all these years of demonstrating, it still gives us a wonderful feeling inside when we see the portrait and photo side by side... its as if spirit are saying "look I'm still here", we both know how privileged and honoured we are to be used as channels for spirit.

We have included in this book just a few examples of the many spirit people that have drawn close over the years; one portrait was drawn during a service at Sheerness Spiritualist Church, in Kent many years ago. In those days we used to sketch the portraits of spirit people onto paper, but now we place them on a projector and screen (6x4) so that at bigger demonstrations people at the back can see them clearly.

Sometimes Tony feels spirit people draw close to him in the afternoon before the service (some spirit people are so impatience!) On these occasions we normally sit quietly together (meditative state) in our group room, and invite those from the world of spirit to draw even closer so Tony can sketch their portraits, and I can help add any messages that they want written on the side, such as dates and names etc.

We have included one of the spirit portraits that was sketched in the afternoon before a service we were taking at Aberdare Spiritualist Church in the Welsh Valleys, we have placed the photo that the lovely lady sent to us in the book for comparison.

Spirit portrait drawn at Sheerness with a photograph for comparison

Spirit portrait sketched at Aberdare, Wales, 2005 with a comparison photo

CHAPTER 14

Teacher Chang Guide and Mentor

As you know I have mention my good friend and guide "Chang" many times and I feel it is time to write about him, he would like that, you could say that he has just given me permission.

I first saw him many years ago when he appeared to me, I was about 10yrs of age, such an old wrinkled fella! Sorry Chang! With wisps of hair falling down his face and neck he looked so wise with a twinkle in his eyes and smiling as if saying "You know me my little one" his pet name for me ever since, his description I remember well, a beautiful white misty light surrounded him, I didn't feel any fear whatsoever, but what I did feel was ever so humble, and surrounded by an over powering love, I could not open my mouth to speak, for I just knew that this was a very special spirit person, although no words were actually spoken, it was as if we heard each others thoughts and knew we were talking!

He was certainly not of this world, this age, or this generation much, much later I was to find out exactly who this special spiritual person was and how our lives are forever intertwined. I was aware of his name from this very first meeting he was not English, and must come from another part of the world, one of my first thoughts was that he might be my granddad? But he didn't look like any member of our family, that I knew of, this was the first of many such visit that my good friend "Chang" made to me, he became like another father, constantly talking and teaching me lessons that were some times easy, (if I listened) but usually I had to learn them my way, the hard way! You silly girl Ann!

Often I would dream of him, and he was always in this building that some how seemed familiar to me, there were others with him dressed in long gowns all kneeling and praying as people do in temples! As I grew up and went through, like many of us do, human lessons, he didn't seem to visit so often, well if he did I wasn't really aware of it. I always felt that he was there in the back ground. I never stopped dreaming of him, and learnt much of his life, and the fact that we were some how related, a feeling that has been with me from our first encounter! I knew that I was his niece, many hundreds of years ago in China, and we lived on this beautiful mountain. Chang was born around 2000 years ago, he was a kind of Taoist monk, and he was very friendly with the Emperor of that era, eventually the emperor gave permission for Chang to practise his own very modern ideas, and mystical gifts, building an entire empire of the third Taoist Dynasty temples, he became known as "Heavenly Teacher Chang" in and around Shanghai, and all over China.

He loved and helped the poor, at every opportunity given, as did his many ordained priests/monks. He lived on Dragon/Tiger Mountain where to this day his family generation after generation has carried on his noble work! His very modem teachings, and ideas of the mystical matters, were very much in line with 20th century thinking.

Although I still do not know all about "Chang" and his earthly life I really don't feel that this is important, what is important is the fact that he has stood beside me all of these years sharing his vast knowledge and philosophy of spirit and life with a simplicity that a child would understand, when I go into a state of trance he draws close and overshadows me, using me as his Spiritual Channel, he does so using the old yoga system of years and years gone by! What is it that they say, out with the old and in with the new! I don't think so!

I thank you "Chang" for guiding me, teaching me, and for always being there for me.

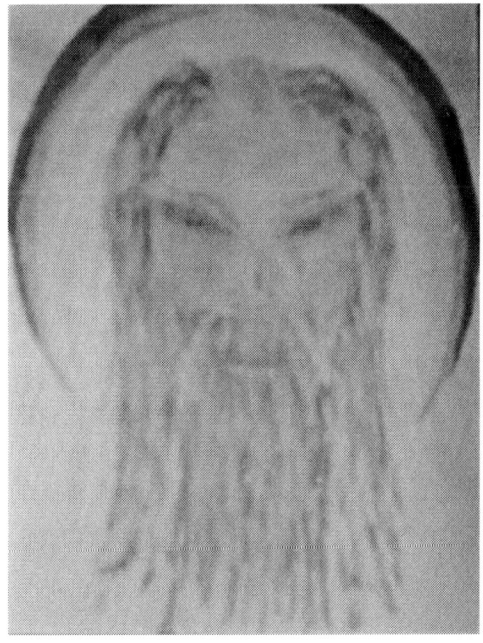

EPILOGUE

Tony and I have for many years, taken our holidays in Wales a most beautiful and magical part of the British Isles, we always take our pussy cats with us in our camper-van, as they also like the change of scenery any way if we didn't take them they would sulk with us for ages! There's some thing about Wales and the people that as always pulled us, so one day after I had retired, (pensioner now) we upped sticks, and moved lock stock and barrel to Wales that was in October 2003 and we haven't looked back since. Spiritually it has been one of the most amazing times, meeting so many wonderful and gifted spiritual people, and having the privilege to serve some truly genuine Spiritualist Churches, we are both sure that in time spirit will make it clear to us why they inspired us to move to Wales, but even if they chose not to it won't bother us because, we are well and truly settled and extremely happy living here and feel as if we have at last come home.

It has been a pleasure for us both to share our little book of factual spiritual experiences with you; and we only hope that your own individual spiritual and life's journey brings you as much happiness and joy as ours has so far, watch this space as book two is being written as we speak.